DY

Joining Forces
a study of links between special and ordinary schools

Joining Forces
a study of links between
special and ordinary schools

Sandra Jowett
Seamus Hegarty
and
Diana Moses

NFER-NELSON

Published by The NFER-NELSON Publishing Company Ltd.,
Darville House, 2 Oxford Road East,
Windsor, Berkshire SL4 1DF, England.

First Published 1988
© 1988, National Foundation for Educational Research

Typeset by First Page Ltd., Watford.
Printed by Billing & Sons Ltd., Worcester.

ISBN 0 7005 1179 2 (Hardback)
Code 8297 02 1

ISBN 0 7005 1162 8 (Paperback)
Code 8292 02 1

Contents

The National Foundation for Educational Research

The National Foundation for Educational Research in England and Wales was founded in 1946 and is Britain's leading educational research institution. It is an independent body undertaking research and development projects on issues of current interest in all sectors of the public educational system. Its membership includes all the local education authorities in England and Wales, the main teachers' associations, and a large number of other major organizations with educational interests.

Its approach is scientific, apolitical and non-partisan. By means of research projects and extensive field surveys it has provided objective evidence on important educational issues for the use of teachers, administrators, parents and the research community. The expert and experienced staff that has been built up over the years enables the Foundation to make use of a wide range of modern research techniques, and, in addition to its own work, it undertakes a large number of specially sponsored projects at the request of government departments and other agencies.

The major part of the research programme relates to the maintained educational sector – primary, secondary and further education. A further significant element has to do specifically with local education authorities and training institutions. The current programme includes work on the education of pupils with special needs, monitoring of pupil performance, staff development, national evaluation and major curriculum programmes, test development, and information technology in schools. The Foundation is also the national agency for a number of international research and information exchange networks.

The NFER-NELSON Publishing Company are the main publishers of the Foundation's research reports. These reports are now available in the *NFER Research Library*, a collection which provides the educational community with up-to-date research into a wide variety of subject areas. In addition, the Foundation and NFER-NELSON work closely together to provide a wide range of open and closed educational tests and a test advisory service. NFER-NELSON also publish *Educational Research*, the termly journal of the Foundation.

Acknowledgements

The authors would like to thank all the headteachers who responded to our questionnaires on links involving their schools. The staff in the nine case study schools and the ordinary schools they linked with provided the team with a great deal of information and their hospitality is appreciated. We are grateful to the pupils who talked so fully to us about their experiences and to the parents we interviewed who welcomed us into their homes. The comments and support of members of the DES Steering Committee were valuable. Wendy Keys and Shirley Cleave at the National Foundation for Education Research read the first draft with meticulous care and made useful contributions to the final product. Professor Ronald Gulliford's constructive advice was welcomed. The typing was very efficiently executed by Moci Carter, Annie Cridge and Jane Lever.

The research was funded by the Department of Education and Science.

1   Background to the Study

Special schooling in context

Special schools are a significant part of special educational provision in Britain, as in most developed countries. For many years they were the only access to formal education for a sizeable number of children and young people. The early special schools, which were established during the nineteenth century, focused on children with physical and sensory impairments. Further schools were set up in the early years of the twentieth century. The post-war expansion in education touched special education also, if not always in the most positive ways. The number of special schools in England and Wales virtually doubled between 1945 and 1971 (from 528 to 1019). The last big growth in special school numbers was in 1971–72 when all children became the responsibility of the education authorities. Children and young people previously deemed ineducable were now to go to school and be educated. They were transferred from junior training centres and some 400 new special schools were established.

Since 1972 the number of special schools has been relatively static. There have been major developments in special education during this period. Some of these, such as the efforts to integrate pupils with special needs, have led to special schools being closed; others, such as ordinary schools' growing reluctance to educate pupils with emotional and behavioural difficulties, have resulted in increased special school provision. The net effect is that the number of special schools has stayed broadly in step with the size of the school-going population. The number of special school pupils aged 5–15 as a proportion of the total school population has been a fairly constant 13 per thousand.

There are currently close on 1600 special schools in England and Wales providing education for 120,000 pupils. They employ more than 17,000 teachers as well as numerous other staff. They have considerable capital assets. While some older buildings may be substandard, many special schools have been built and fitted out to a high standard.

A large number have lifts, swimming pools, soundproofed rooms or other specialist areas and equipment as appropriate.

Special schools are clearly a major resource in the education of pupils with special needs. They have, moreover, made significant contributions to the practice of special education. They have, for instance, promoted interdisciplinary working and pioneered new pedagogical techniques. They now, however, face a watershed in their development. On the one hand, new roles are being thrust upon them, whereas on the other hand, the rationale for their very existence is being questioned.

Regardless of the pressures toward desegregation and the aspirations to build up provision in ordinary schools, special schools are going to be part of the pattern of provision for some time to come. Even if it were not evident that progress toward the necessary reform of the ordinary school is slow, it must be remembered that the special school sector is a complex system of educational provision. It is not possible to dismantle it overnight and re-establish equivalent provision in ordinary schools. System change needs time and should be consolidated on the basis of lessons learned from experience.

Toward links

The pragmatist's response to this situation is to ask how ordinary schools can capitalize on this resource. Special schools have precisely what, at the moment, many ordinary schools are lacking – expertise in teaching pupils with special educational needs. The best special schools have a developed competence in modifying and implementing the curriculum for pupils who learn with difficulty, and ordinary schools can only gain from tapping into this experience. Hence, the purpose of the present study has been to examine the ways in which special schools and ordinary schools can work together for the benefit of pupils.

The idea of cooperation between special schools and ordinary schools is not a new one. The Warnock Report (1978) commended a number of experiments designed to secure closer cooperation. It went on to endorse the practice in the strongest terms. It recommended that 'firm links should be established between special and ordinary schools in the same vicinity' (8.10). These should include, as appropriate, educational programmes, social experiences and resources. Such links, if successfully planned, benefit pupils and teachers alike. Pupils gain through curriculum enrichment and more natural participation in social activities. Teachers in ordinary schools benefit from the expertise of colleagues in special schools while the latter avoid the professional isolation experienced by many in special schools.

The Warnock Report commended in particular the practice of designating some special schools in each local authority as resource centres, i.e. 'centres of specialist expertise and of research in special education, in which teachers in the area would be closely involved' (8.13). Such centres should have a wide remit, encompassing curriculum development, in-service education, information giving and the lending of specialized materials and equipment. The facilities should be available to parents as well as to professionals. Several local authorities have in fact laid down policy guidelines to further this and other forms of cooperation between special schools and ordinary schools.

The research

The study of link arrangements reported here was part of a larger study of support for ordinary schools in meeting special educational needs. This was conducted at the National Foundation for Educational Research between autumn 1983 and summer 1986. The study was funded by the Department of Education and Science as one of three supported by the Department in the wake of the Education Act 1981. The other projects were conducted at the University of London Institute of Education and, jointly, the University of Manchester and Huddersfield Polytechnic. The findings of the latter have been reported in Robson *et al.* (1988).

The NFER study grew out of a concern that primary and secondary schools were having to take on a range of tasks for which they were neither resourced nor prepared. Previous research at the NFER had highlighted the importance of adequate support for ordinary schools if they were to provide an appropriate education for pupils with special educational needs. It was accordingly decided to focus on the theme of support for the ordinary school in meeting special educational needs. Three aspects of support were singled out for scrutiny and these became the three prongs of the study:

  1 Local authority support services. Schools need encouragement, advice and resources from their local authority. The early 1980s saw considerable development in support

services – existing services were restructured or expanded, and new ones were established. Information on the emerging patterns of support was collected and its impact on schools analysed.

2 In-service training and professional development. Meeting special educational needs in the ordinary school on the scale envisaged here calls for nothing less than a reform of the ordinary school system. This must be matched by a corresponding reform in training. There is currently a proliferation of training initiatives within both training institutions and local authorities. Information was gathered on these initiatives and their implications for schools.

3 Links between special schools and ordinary schools. Reports on 1 and 2 are available in the companion volumes by Moses *et al.* (1988) and Hegarty and Moses (1988).

For the purposes of the study, links were assumed to be any sharing of pupils, staff or material resources between special schools and ordinary schools. The sharing could be in either direction and could be one-way only or reciprocal. It could be confined to a single element, e.g. pupils, or it could involve an integrated package of all three.

There are two separate elements to the research reported here: a questionnaire survey of all the special schools in a quarter of the local education authorities in England and Wales concerning any contacts they may have with ordinary schools; and a series of detailed case studies of nine well-established link schemes. In addition, visits were made to a large number of special schools in England and Wales.

While information from the questionnaires documents the extent to which special schools were involved in contacts with ordinary schools and the form that these took, the detailed case studies allow for a more general discussion of the practice and potential of this form of organization. Preliminary visits to a large number of schools were undertaken and on the basis of these and other sources of information available, nine schools were selected for detailed investigation. Information was collected in the case study schools on the perspectives of teachers, headteachers and, in some instances, pupils and parents. Interviews were also conducted with educational psychologists, education officers and advisers concerned with pupils with special needs. This information shows how the present arrangements work and indicates the long-term implications for special schools. By drawing together the two elements in the research, it is hoped that a comprehensive account of the links formed between special schools and ordinary schools emerges.

The findings from the survey are presented in Chapter 2, showing the extent of link arrangements of different kinds. This quantitative picture is complemented in Chapter 3 by a detailed account of links in action. Nine links are described in order to give a flavour of what they are like in practice for the pupils and staff involved. Chapters 4 and 5 describe the setting up of links schemes and administering them once established. The next two chapters spell out the implications for teachers, pupils and parents. Chapter 8 considers the implications of link schemes for some aspects of special education and the final chapter places links in the context of the future development of special schools.

2 The Nature and Extent of Links between Special and Ordinary Schools

The survey

Twenty-six local education authorities, a quarter of the total in England and Wales, were selected using random number tables, and all their special schools were sent a questionnaire in the summer term of 1985. This sought information about the nature and extent of any links they had with ordinary schools. Two hundred and ninety eight schools were approached in this way and asked either to complete the questionnaire or to return the slip enclosed stating that they were not currently involved in any links with ordinary schools. The questionnaire was divided into two sections, one recording movement *from* the special schools and the other reporting movement *to* them, in relation to staff, pupils and resources.

Information is available from this survey about the extent and purpose of the movement of staff between special and ordinary schools, the extent of movement of pupils, in both directions, in groups and individually, the sharing of resources and the possible development of links as described by the special school headteachers. A total of 268 replies was obtained, giving a response rate of 90 per cent. The links documented on the questionnaires varied greatly in their scope and purpose. Some small-scale schemes had little impact on the participating schools, while others entailed substantial movement of staff and pupils which affected the schools' structure and day-to-day running in significant ways. Information from the questionnaires is presented separately in relation to the movement of staff, pupils and resources, and in each section movement from the special school is described before that occurring in the other direction.

The schools

The 268 schools responding to the questionnaire catered for children with a variety of special educational needs. There were 21 schools for physically handicapped pupils, 45 for those with behaviour problems, 96 for pupils with severe and 91 for pupils with moderate learning difficulties. The 15 schools in the other category used in this chapter catered for those with sensory impairments, communication disorders or for a wide spectrum of pupils with special needs. These figures are presented in Table 2.1.

Table 2.1: *Types of special schools responding to the questionnaire*

Schools for	Number of schools	%
Pupils with physical handicaps	21	8
Pupils with severe learning difficulties	96	36
Pupils with behaviour problems	45	17
Pupils with moderate learning difficulties	91	34
Pupils with other special needs	15	5
	268	100

There were 197 headteachers who reported that their schools were involved in a link of one sort or another and 26 who were in the process of developing some arrangements with ordinary schools. Only 40 schools (15 per cent) replying to the questionnaire did not have plans or past experience or current arrangements in relation to link schemes. These figures are presented in Table 2.2.

Table 2.2: *Special schools involved in links*

	Number of schools	%
Current link	197	73
Plans for a link	26	10
Previous link	5	2
No involvement in links	40	15
	268	100

A breakdown of current links by type of special school is presented in Table 2.3. It is of interest that schools for pupils with severe learning difficulties had the highest proportion of links, with eight out of ten reporting a current link. Schools for pupils with physical handicaps had the smallest proportion, though two-thirds of such schools did in fact report a link.

Table 2.3:   *Types of special school reporting current links*

Schools for	Number of schools	% of type of school
Pupils with physical handicaps	14	67
Pupils with severe learning difficulties	77	80
Pupils with behaviour problems	31	69
Pupils with moderate learning difficulties	64	70
Pupils with other special needs	11	73
	197	

Staff involvement in link schemes

Staff going *from* the special school

Headteachers answering the questionnaire were asked how many teachers and ancillaries were involved in link schemes, how regular their involvement was, how much time they spent in ordinary schools and what activities they engaged in while they were there. Table 2.4 shows that two-thirds of the special schools sampled had staff going to an ordinary school, either on a regular weekly basis or less frequently. Naturally, the purpose and duration of this contact varied a great deal. Schools which did have contact tended to divide fairly evenly between those who had regular weekly involvement and those who had irregular involvement only. Staff who had regular contact were engaged in a wide range of activities, whereas those having less frequent contact were largely taken up with liaising over particular pupils with special needs.

Table 2.4:   *Special schools with staff involvement in ordinary schools*

	No. of special schools	%
Regular weekly involvement	95	35
Less regular involvement	84	32
No involvement	89	33
	268	100

Both teachers and ancillaries were involved in links. Table 2.5 shows how they were distributed in schools where there was at least weekly contact. Teachers were involved in most cases and, in more than half the schools, only teachers were involved. The number of teachers involved per school ranged from one to eight, with an average of just over two. (The average number of teachers in a special school is approximately 11, so this represents one teacher in five in the schools with links.) The average number of ancillaries going out from a special school was just under two. The 86 schools where teachers were regularly involved had 200 teachers spending time in ordinary schools, and 83 ancillaries were taking part in links from 45 schools.

Table 2.5: *The distribution of special school teachers and ancillari es in weekly contact with ordinary schools*

	No. of special schools	%
Both teachers and ancillaries participating	36	38
Teachers only	50	53
Ancillaries only	9	9
	95	100

Most of these teachers were spending relatively short periods of time each week in an ordinary school. Table 2.6 shows that 60 per cent were spending less than three hours a week, and a further 16 per cent spent between three and five hours in other schools. For this group of teachers the link scheme remained a small part of their working week. As against that, a quarter were working outside their own school for one or more days a week and in a few cases were spending the entire week working in other schools.

A similar pattern of time allocation was found for the 83 ancillaries: 64 (77 per cent) went out for less than three hours a week, 15 for three to five hours and four on a full-time basis. In the vast majority of cases these ancillaries were described as 'accompanying' pupils from the special schools. The four who spent a full timetable in an ordinary school were providing welfare support for secondary age pupils with physical handicaps from one school. One assistant was spending 2½ hours a week attending an in-service course at an ordinary school. As noted above, 83 ancillaries went out from 45 schools. This amounted to a sixth of the special schools sampled. The movement was still of interest, however, particularly when the smaller number of ancillary staff in schools is taken into account.

Table 2.6: *Time spent in ordinary schools by special school teachers each week*

	No. of teachers	%
Less than 3 hours	119	60
3–5 hours	32	16
6–15 hours	36	18
16–25 hours	6	3
25+ hours	7	3
	200	100

What did special school teachers do in ordinary schools? Table 2.7 shows that teaching accounted for two-thirds of the activities reported. The table is based on 200 teachers but the total number of activities is greater than this since several teachers took part in more than one activity. This section describes how the teachers' time was divided up in ordinary schools. Chapter 6 returns to this topic and develops the implications for practice. Teaching clearly predominated, with the most frequently occurring activity being the teaching of groups containing pupils from both the ordinary and the special school. The next most frequent activity was advising colleagues in the ordinary school on matters relating to teaching and handling pupils with special needs; this accounted for nearly a third of the activities reported. The other main activity, accounting for just under a fifth of reported activities, was teaching groups comprised exclusively of pupils from the special school in an ordinary school.

A distinction can be drawn between support from the special school related specifically to individual pupils who move over as part of their timetable and support which comes in the form of a service from the special school. The former is directly related to pupils coming from the special school whereas the latter is concerned with general support and guidance for staff in ordinary schools. An example of the first is the teacher who spends three hours a week 'advising on the feasibility of integration and arranging individual placements'; and an example of the second is the teacher who spends two hours a week 'advising teachers how to tackle specific behaviour problems, i.e. setting up behaviour modification programmes'.

The teaching undertaken by the special school teachers in ordinary schools took a number of forms. In addition to teaching combined groups, they also taught groups comprised exclusively of pupils from the special school or – less commonly – ordinary school classes which did not contain any special school pupils. Examples of the different arrangements are: (a) a teacher who spent one hour a week taking an integrated music and singing session, (b) another who spent 1½ hours a week teaching keyboard skills to physically handicapped pupils, and (c) another who had a full-time teaching commitment to pupils in the ordinary school, particularly those in the lower ability range. As noted, some teachers spent time on more than one activity; one teacher, for example, spent 1¼ hours a week working with a pupil with cerebral palsy and the rest of her time in that school discussing progress and difficulties with the teacher or welfare assistant involved.

Table 2.7:   Work undertaken by special school teachers in ordinary schools each week

	No. of activities	%
Teaching pupils from the special school	39	18
Teaching pupils from the ordinary school	10	5
Teaching combined groups	89	42
Advising colleagues	61	29
Liaising about pupil placements	12	6
	*211	100

*a small number of the 200 teachers undertook more than one activity

The figures presented so far show the extent to which members of staff from special schools spent time in ordinary schools as part of their regular timetables and what the purposes of their visits were. Some detail was also provided in the questionnaires about the work undertaken. This is presented in Tables 2.8 and 2.9 in relation to different types of special school.

Table 2.8:   Time spent by special school teachers in ordinary schools each week

Teachers from schools for	Amount of time					Number of teachers
	less than 3 hrs	3–5 hrs	6–15 hrs	16–25 hrs	25+ hrs	
Pupils with physical handicaps	10	2	2	–	2	16
Pupils with severe learning difficulties	76	13	5	1	–	95
Pupils with behaviour problems	4	4	6	–	2	16
Pupils with moderate learning difficulties	25	11	11	1	–	48
Pupils with other special needs	6	1	12	3	3	25
						200

Table 2.9: *Work undertaken by special school teachers in ordinary schools each week*

Teachers from schools for	Activities					
	Teaching pupils from the special school	*Teaching pupils from the ordinary school*	*Teaching combined groups*	*Advising colleagues*	*Liaising*	*Number of activities**
Pupils with physical handicaps	5	–	6	1	4	16
Pupils with severe learning difficulties	16	–	67	9	3	95
Pupils with behaviour problems	3	6	3	8	3	23
Pupils with moderate learning difficulties	8	5	3	31	1	48
Pupils with other special needs	5	–	8	15	1	29
						211

* a small number of the 200 teachers undertook more than one activity

Schools for pupils with physical handicaps

Nearly a third of these 21 schools had links involving staff, with 16 teachers and 18 ancillaries taking part. Two-thirds of the teachers spent less than three hours a week in ordinary schools and two were involved on a full-time basis. Teaching was the main activity, evenly divided between integrated groups and groups from the special school. There were four instances of staff liaising about individual pupils and just one of advisory work with colleagues. Three-quarters of the 18 ancillaries who took part in links were attending for less than three hours, one was out for five hours, and the other four worked in ordinary schools for the whole of their timetable.

The most substantial staff involvement was at a school where two teachers spent 25 hours a week providing general support to pupils with physical handicaps and four assistants provided support for two hours each. Twenty pupils from this school spent between three and five hours a week in ordinary schools, 20 had 1½ hour weekly placements, and there was regular movement of pupils from the ordinary school to the special school for specific teaching. The headteacher commented that 'the area you are researching in relation to our school is vast. This is rapidly becoming a major part of our work'. A different scheme existed at another school where two teachers spent 15 hours a week advising on the full-time integration of 23 pupils and the part-time placement of a further 16. Teachers at this school undertook a range of work in that one spent 1½ hours teaching a special needs pupil, one spent four hours accompanying a group for social integration and another was supervising children using the ordinary school swimming pool for two hours. Four ordinary schools were involved, and there were plans to have more staff visiting the receiving schools to give teaching support.

Schools for pupils with severe learning difficulties

Half of the 96 schools participating in this survey had links involving staff, with 95 teachers and 57 ancillaries taking part. In six links, only ancillaries were involved. Most of the teachers spent less than three hours in ordinary schools and only six were out for more than six hours. None of the ancillaries spent more than four hours in ordinary schools. The main purpose of the links was for staff to participate in integrated sessions with pupils from their school; nearly three-quarters of the visits took this form. Six teachers, for example, worked for between one and five hours a week teaching art and craft, social education, PE and drama to integrated groups in ordinary schools. The next biggest commitment was to teach pupils with special needs and 16 teachers did this. Another three were liaising about individual pupils and nine were acting in an advisory capacity.

Three teachers from one school each visited up to six ordinary schools for six or eight hours a week to provide support to primary schools having pupils with special needs. They were in effect providing a service designed to assess the needs of individual pupils with learning difficulties, to assist teachers in developing appropriate programmes, to provide resources and enable teachers in ordinary schools to have a better understanding of the problems of pupils with learning difficulties. It was envisaged that one teacher already spending six hours in the scheme would have three-quarters of her timetable allocated to this support work. The largest amount of time in an ordinary school was spent by a teacher who worked three days a week with a senior class in their base at the nearby comprehensive school. These seven pupils spent 19½ hours a week on the ordinary school site. For welfare assistants, the time spent in ordinary schools was not a substantial element in their working week. Only one assistant, who spent four hours a week out, was involved for more than three hours.

Schools for pupils with behaviour problems

Nearly a quarter of the 45 schools had links involving members of staff, with 16 teachers and two ancillaries taking part. The two ancillaries spent two hours a week in ordinary schools and were the only members of staff involved in link schemes from their school. Half of the teachers spent less than five hours a week in ordinary schools, six were involved for between six and 15 hours, and two were working in ordinary schools on a full-time basis. The most common activity, undertaken by a third of the teachers, was advising colleagues in ordinary schools. A quarter of the teachers taught ordinary school classes.

The movement of staff from schools for pupils with behaviour problems is complicated by the fact that schools may be actively but sporadically involved in the re-integration of pupils, and this may not be reflected in the regular weekly movement figures. Thirteen schools specifically referred to the contacts made as a result of returning, or introducing, pupils to ordinary schools, and the arrangements to facilitate this varied considerably. A small number of schools for pupils with behaviour problems were providing boarding accommodation for some pupils who attended nearby schools full-time.

Of the two teachers with a full-time commitment outside the special school, one was engaged in supporting pupils moving out of the special school and the other taught classes in the ordinary school. Seven schools specifically referred to plans being formulated to develop outreach work, and two schemes were to commence in the following September. One headteacher enclosed a detailed discussion document outlining outreach procedures and goals. This proposed that 'Given or having appropriate qualifications, interest and expertise, special school staff might offer advice about early identification of special needs, adjusting the curriculum, working with parents, teaching methods and equipment and about the implications of different handicaps'.

Schools for pupils with moderate learning difficulties

Nearly a quarter of the 91 schools were organizing the regular weekly movement of staff. In two cases this involved ancillaries only and in three instances both teachers and ancillaries took part. None of the ancillaries spent more than two hours a week engaged in this work. Of the 48 teachers coming from these special schools, half were out for less than three hours, one teacher worked full-time in the ordinary school and the remainder were spending between half a day and two days out. In two-thirds of the links, teachers were advising colleagues in ordinary schools. Apart from one liaison link, all the other teachers were teaching.

In one school a Scale 3 teacher spent four days a week visiting mainstream schools to 'help teachers design suitable work programmes, change class organisation and methodology, etc.'. Another teacher at this school was engaged in similar work for three hours a week. Another school had a slightly different arrangement involving five teachers. Three of them offered guidance about curriculum development and assessment for 12, 12 and nine hours respectively. Another teacher was working with colleagues in ordinary schools to develop a leavers' programme, and another worked alongside pupils from the special school who were spending half a day a week in classes in ordinary schools.

Other special schools

Two-thirds of the 15 schools in this category had links involving staff, with 25 teachers taking part. A quarter of these teachers were out for less than three hours a week, half for between one and two days, and the rest for more than two days. Of these, three were out on a full-time basis. Between them they reported 29 activities in ordinary schools, with the provision of specialist advice and support accounting for more than half of these.

One school acted as a base for specialist staff in the local authority working with hearing impaired and visually impaired pupils. Eight teachers spent time working outside the school, three for 20 hours each to support pupils with sensory impairments, one for 12 hours to develop pupils' communication skills, one for four hours to advise on computer use, and three for six hours each to provide advice and support in relation to educating pupils with visual impairments. Another school sent one teacher out for 15 hours a week to teach pupils with Statements and to provide advice to teachers in ordinary schools. Three teachers from another school went out for 20, 15 and 12 hours respectively to advise teachers on strategies for pupils with any sort of learning difficulty. The link in another involved one teacher spending three half-days accompanying one pupil to classes in an ordinary school.

While their involvement in link schemes was not substantially altering the working lives of many of the teachers involved, a minority were experiencing a significant change in their work, the implications of which will be explored in Chapter 6. Information was also collected about teachers moving out from their schools on a less regular basis; 84 schools (31 per cent) reported less than weekly staff contact with ordinary schools. This was very largely concerned with liaising about individual pupils from the special school.

Breaking down the activities undertaken by teachers into the groupings shown above illustrates the rationales for establishing these links. Teaching was the main activity for teachers from schools for pupils with physical handicaps and for pupils with severe learning difficulties. Most of these teachers spent short periods of time in the ordinary schools they visited. Staff from the latter group were usually accompanying groups of their pupils for integrated sessions in ordinary schools. Providing support for their colleagues in ordinary schools was the main task for teachers from schools for pupils with moderate learning difficulties. This was also a large part of the work of teachers from schools for pupils with behaviour problems and those catering for a variety of needs in the 'other' category used above. Two-thirds of this last group of schools had staff going out to ordinary schools as did half of those for pupils with severe learning difficulties.

Staff going *to* the special school

Teachers

There were 103 special school headteachers (38 per cent) in this survey who reported that there was some movement of teachers to their schools, and in a quarter of cases this was regular weekly contact. The details are presented in Table 2.10. Just over half of these weekly arrangements were enabling teachers in ordinary schools to benefit from resources available at the special school or to draw on the experience of special school staff. One headteacher, for example, reported that 'four teachers come weekly to look at individual programme work, observe children and discuss equipment' and another that 'four teachers will visit weekly on average. They will observe teaching techniques, study record keeping and individual learning programmes, collect reference materials, borrow teaching materials and toys and use computers in the classroom'.

The rest of the weekly contacts involved direct work with pupils. One headteacher wrote: 'Two teachers come weekly to school. One is team teaching and another is supporting pupil placement in special school classes.' Another described an arrangement whereby two teachers visited the school weekly to work in a senior class and 'to develop professional skills by team teaching'. This contact with pupils on a regular basis was timetabled activity for the teachers involved, whereas the visits for resources referred to above might involve different teachers every week.

In the 77 schools that had less than weekly staff contact, a variety of activities were undertaken. There were 12 references to meetings to liaise about pupils who were attending two schools. Such visits were invariably described as 'occasional' and 'ad hoc'. Eleven schools had open days for staff from ordinary schools. One school for pupils with

Table 2.10:   *Visits by ordinary school teachers to special schools*

	Number of schools	%
Weekly visits	26	10
Less frequent visits	77	29
No visits	165	61
	268	100

behaviour problems ran a 'Troublesome Kids' group on the first Tuesday of the month attended by between ten and 30 mainstream teachers. Another school had invited all primary headteachers in the area to evening meetings to establish contact because 'successful reintegration occurs at primary level'. A school for pupils with moderate learning difficulties had hosted several workshops and joint meetings for ordinary schools. Videos produced at the school about teaching programmes were available on loan and biannual 'At Homes' were held when primary and secondary teachers were invited to see the work and resources on offer to them. A small group of teachers from ordinary schools visited one special school to work on a long-term curriculum development project for secondary age pupils.

Ancillaries

There were 12 special schools that had classroom assistants coming to them and in all but two instances this was regular weekly contact. Two special schools ran short training courses for newly appointed assistants in ordinary schools. Most of the regular contact entailed working with pupils, usually alongside their classroom teacher. One school had six teachers and one assistant visiting weekly to accompany pupils to the swimming pool, and another had an assistant coming weekly to work with a special school teacher and a 'mixed' group of pupils. There was one instance of an assistant visiting a special school weekly for 'resources, advice and training'.

Pupil involvement in link schemes

Pupils going *from* the special school

Just over half (144) of the special schools surveyed had pupils going out to other schools on a regular weekly basis, while 15 schools (five per cent) reported contact of a less frequent kind. Eight respondents made points concerning the movement of pupils that was not on a regular basis but was clearly of significance. A typical response from a school with ad hoc arrangements was from the headteacher of a school for pupils with behaviour problems who said that between eight and ten pupils had returned to ordinary schools over the last four years. More than a third of schools were not organizing any pupil movement. These figures are given in Table 2.11.

Table 2.11:   *Pupil movement from special to ordinary schools*

	Number of schools	*%*
Regular weekly contact	144	54
Less regular contact	15	5
Ad hoc arrangements	8	3
No contact	101	38
	268	100

In 122 of the 144 schools where weekly links were arranged, pupils went out to ordinary schools on an individual basis. In 68 schools, pupils' link programmes were arranged on a group basis. There was overlap here in that some of the 144 special schools involved were sending both groups and individual pupils. Individual placements accounted for 597 pupils. There were 74 groups, comprising 1008 pupils. (Some of the 68 'group' schools sent more than one group.) Where special schools organized individual placements, the number of pupils per school was typically small: nearly three-quarters of the 122 schools involved had five pupils or fewer in link programmes. Group links tended to involve larger numbers from a given school: two-thirds of the special school groups going out to ordinary schools contained six or more pupils, in some cases considerably more. The details are given in Table 2.12.

Table 2.12:   *Pupils going from special to ordinary schools*

	Individual pupils			Groups	
Number of pupils	*Number of special schools*	*%*	*Size of group*	*Number of groups*	*%*
less than 3	55	45	less than 3	7	9
3–5	33	27	3–5	16	23
6–15	27	22	6–15	35	47
16–25	5	4	16–25	9	12
25+	2	2	25+	7	9
	122	100		74	100

The amount of time that special school pupils spent in ordinary schools was related to whether they were attending individually or as members of a group. More than half of the pupils on individual placements spent at least one day a week in ordinary schools, whereas most of the groups (81 per cent) were out for less than three hours. Only a fifth of the pupils attending classes on an individual basis were out for less than three hours. This disparity reflects the different rationales and aims of the pupils' attendance. Pupils going out in groups to extend their social experience and participate in integrated sessions spent a short period of time in other schools. Those going individually for particular subjects, perhaps with a view to full-time integration, would be timetabled for longer periods in the ordinary school. The figures for the time spent in ordinary schools are detailed in Table 2.13.

Table 2.13: *The amount of time spent by pupils in ordinary schools each week*

Amount of time	Individual pupils		Groups of pupils	
	number	%	*number*	%
less than 3 hours	113	19	60	81
3–5 hours	171	29	10	14
6–15 hours	157	26	2	3
16–25 hours	32	5	1	1
25+ hours	124	21	1	1
	597	100	74	100

Some special schools were organizing time for their pupils in ordinary schools that changed the working arrangements of both the pupils and the schools involved. The figures for the regular weekly movement of pupils were analysed in relation to the impact the links had on the pupils' timetable (Table 2.14). In more than half of the 144 schools where pupils were going out regularly, at least one pupil was spending a full school day or more in another school. In almost a quarter of them, at least one pupil was spending between half a day and a full day out, and in the others pupils were involved for less than half a school day. The hours that pupils spent in other schools were also considered in terms of the organizational demands placed on the staff who were making the arrangements. As is shown in Table 2.14, a fifth of schools were making arrangements for more than 70 pupil hours to be spent in other schools and another fifth organized between 31 and 70 hours.

Table 2.14: *Impact of pupil movement from special to ordinary schools*

On pupils' timetables		
Amount of time	*Number of schools*	*%*
At least one pupil for at least one day	75	52
At least one pupil for between half and one day	34	24
At least one pupil for less than half a day	35	24
	144	100

On school organization		
Number of 'pupil hours'	*Number of schools*	*%*
More than 70 hours (about 11 pupil days)	31	22
31–70 hours (5–10 pupil days)	32	22
Less than 30 hours (less than 5 pupil days)	81	56
	144	100

Thus, nearly half of the schools were organizing more than 30 'pupil hours' each week and a similar proportion had at least one pupil attending an ordinary school for at least one full day. More than a fifth of pupils attending on an individual basis were spending most of their time in an ordinary school. One school for pupils with physical handicaps, for example, had 23 pupils attending ordinary schools on this basis. Five teachers spent varying amounts of time in these schools, as did five classroom assistants. A school for pupils with behaviour problems had ten pupils attending ordinary schools on a full-time basis. When pupils had been in school for between six months and a year a placement in the ordinary school was considered. A school for pupils with moderate learning difficulties had five children attending ordinary schools for between 16–25 hours and a very flexible arrangement for the transfer of pupils.

Headteachers were asked whether there were procedures for facilitating the transfer of pupils to the ordinary school roll when they spent a considerable amount of time in the ordinary school. This question was not applicable to the majority of situations described in the questionnaire responses, but of the 61 schools where it was, slightly less than half said that arrangements were made for transfer.

Pupils going *to* the special school

The movement of pupils was not exclusively one way. Some 116 special schools had pupils coming to them, and in 81 cases this was on a regular weekly basis. Although headteachers were not asked to elaborate on the purpose of these visits, 90 respondents provided details on how the time in their school was spent: the special school was being used as a resource for pupils on a variety of 'caring' courses in about half of the visits; in a further third of cases, the special schools were providing in some way for pupils with special educational needs in ordinary schools; and in a few cases pupils came for combined sessions or to use resources at the special schools.

A more detailed picture of these pupils' contacts with special schools is provided by separating out schools according to category of special need.

Schools for pupils with physical handicaps

Eleven special schools received pupils from ordinary schools. In six of these pupils were coming individually, and the main purpose of the visits was for pupils to receive specialist services. Forty pupils were involved, and typically a short period of time would be spent in the special school receiving physiotherapy or hydrotherapy. Six schools had pupils coming to them in groups, either as part of their work experience or to benefit from integrated activities. Contact was at least weekly in all but two schools.

Schools for pupils with severe learning difficulties

Pupils came to 64 of these schools and in the majority these were regular weekly visits. In many instances pupils taking courses on caring were coming on placements for practical experience. There were at least four instances of pupils with special needs coming, seven of integrated sessions and three of visits to use the resources of the special schools. One school had run a one-term project dealing with social language and personal development for pupils with special needs, and another took three junior pupils for six hours a week for additional help with their reading.

Schools for pupils with behaviour problems

Five schools had pupils coming to them. In three instances these were occasional, ad hoc visits; in the other two, pupils with special needs were accommodated on a part-time flexible basis.

Schools for pupils with moderate learning difficulties

There were 30 schools that had pupils coming to them, and two-thirds of the visits were organized on a regular weekly basis. In at least 15 cases, pupils with special needs were coming to the school for help in specific areas. There were five schools where secondary school pupils came for placement visits as part of a course, one where they came for integrated sessions and one where their visits were arranged to allow them to use resources at the special school. Some schools reported well established schemes for pupils with special needs. One school, for example, had groups of ten pupils from local primary and secondary schools coming for six-month intensive reading courses. Pupils had to be of average ability and have a specific reading problem. Two pupils came individually to another school for approximately 40 per cent of their timetable – maths, language development and some light craft activities. Twelve pupils also came in groups for 90 minutes a week for an eight-week module of work in the personal and social development programme.

Other special schools

Pupils came to six of these schools, all on a regular weekly basis. Pupil visits ranged from a situation where four pupils came on a permanent part-time basis to develop their basic skills to one where two pupils came for two hours a week typing practice to another where 30 pupils came in groups for integrated games, craft work and nursery activity.

The breakdown of pupils coming to special schools in terms of the type of special school indicates the different reasons for establishing links of this kind. Where schools for pupils with severe learning difficulties were concerned, pupils were coming from other schools mainly as part of a course which required placements. These placement visits were a feature of arrangements in schools for pupils with physical handicaps and those with moderate learning difficulties, but the main purpose of pupil visits in these schools was to secure some form of specialist provision for the visiting pupils. This could be physiotherapy or intensive assistance with reading. Schools for pupils with behaviour problems and those in the 'other' category had pupils coming to them only for specialist support of this kind.

Resources involved in link schemes

Information about the movement and sharing of resources between special and ordinary schools was given by respondents in answer to questions about pupils and staff. Separate questions were included on the questionnaire about the movement of resources, in both directions, and 80 special schools reported that this was a feature of their link arrangement. The most common pattern was for resources to move from the special school to the ordinary school; this is to be expected since the predominant movement of both pupils and staff was in this direction and, indeed, where reverse movement of pupils or staff took place, it was sometimes for the purpose of using fixed resources at the special school. However, in nearly a third of the 80 schools, resources were shared in both directions. Information was not collected about the extent to which resources were used by other schools, but the responses given indicate the potential. Some examples are described below.

> The school provides a back-up facility in terms of paramedical support, teaching advice, equipment, aids etc. Staff training, staff research and reference library, and all contacts are made available.

> We are acting as a local centre for computer software for children with special needs. We make teachers aware of resources and the fact that they can be borrowed.

> A Special Needs Support teacher is based at the school and we are developing a resource bank for special needs pupils in both special and mainstream schools.

Plans

Headteachers were also asked to provide information about any plans they may have had for extending or modifying any existing movements of staff, pupils or resources to and from their schools. Nearly a third referred to some changes envisaged and of these a quarter referred to specific developments due for implementation on a given date. While these proposals must be treated with some caution, they are an indication of interest in the formation and development of links between special and ordinary schools. One headteacher described the new post of an 'integration teacher' to be responsible for the coordination, planning and implementation of links and to provide teaching relief for her colleagues while they took classes. Another school was able to 'offer' three members of staff to ordinary schools; they would work with pupils in infant and junior classes for either one or 1½ days a week.

Summary

Information collected about link schemes from the questionnaire returns showed that a wide variety of arrangements existed. A link between a special and an ordinary school could, for example, result in a group of children from a special school spending time with their teachers in integrated sessions in a neighbouring school that served to extend their social experience. This was a common pattern for links involving children with severe learning difficulties. A link might also involve staff spending a sizeable part of their working week in other schools, where the range of tasks taken on included team teaching, liaising with or advising colleagues and teaching in integrated groups or with withdrawn groups of pupils. There were nine special schools that had links involving teachers only and 52 involved pupils only.

There were 95 special schools (35 per cent) where teachers were regularly spending part of their timetable working in ordinary schools. A third of the teachers' time was spent primarily working with their ordinary school colleagues and two-thirds with pupils. Nearly a quarter of them were spending more than one full day a week engaged in these activities. Eighty-four schools (32 per cent) reported that teachers had contact with staff in ordinary schools on an ad hoc basis, largely concerned with liaising about individual pupils with special needs. One hundred and three special schools in the survey (38 per cent) reported that teachers from ordinary schools visited them, and in a quarter this was regular weekly contact.

More than half of the schools replying to the questionnaire had links that involved the regular weekly movement of pupils, and in more than half of these at least one pupil was spending a full school day or more in another school. When the 'pupil hours' spent in other settings were calculated, it was found that nearly half of the schools were organizing more than 30 'pupil hours' each week. The fact that 85 per cent of respondents had links with other schools or had plans to develop them or had past experience of them shows that arrangements of this kind are a significant feature of special schools. The following chapters will consider the implications of link schemes for those involved, drawing largely on information collected from the nine case study schools.

3 Link Schemes in Action

Nine schools were selected for detailed study over a period of time. They were chosen to represent the range of link schemes in operation. They are spread across six local education authorities, throughout England and Wales. Three of the schools cater for pupils with physical handicaps, two for pupils with moderate learning difficulties, two for those with emotional or behavioural difficulties, one for pupils with severe learning difficulties and one for those with hearing impairment.

The visits made to these schools and the schools they were in contact with generated a substantial amount of the information presented in this report. The issues raised when schools are engaged in links of one sort or another are discussed in the following chapters, as are the implications for those taking part. This chapter describes the special schools that were the focus of the links and the contact they had with other schools.

Powell's Orchard School

This school, catering for pupils with behaviour problems, is situated in the South of England and has approximately 100 pupils part-time and 40 full-time. The numbers fluctuate because the part-time basis on which many children attend means that there is an unusual degree of transfer to and from the roll of the special school. There are four departments, taking pupils from the ages of two to 16, namely the nurture groups, and the junior, secondary and off-site departments. The majority of pupils on the main site have part-time placements and spend the rest of their time in ordinary schools; there is clearly considerable potential for work and liaison with these schools. As well as links involving the part-time pupils in these departments, external groups are run in eight secondary schools by three of the special school staff. Using Powell's Orchard as a base, they establish groups in the schools in conjunction with an ordinary school teacher. Pupils referred to the groups have exhibited minor behaviour problems of one sort or another and placement is designed to provide immediate support for them. They may be shy and withdrawn or the subject of bullying. Most attend the groups for two sessions a week to undertake a variety of activities designed to develop their social and personal skills. The special school teachers act in an advisory capacity, passing on skills and materials to their colleagues in ordinary schools.

The school originally catered for between 40 and 50 pupils on a full-time basis, and the development of part-time placements grew from a concern over the narrow curriculum available for secondary age pupils. It was hoped that all secondary age pupils would have part-time placements and would continue in ordinary schools but this has not been possible in practice. Aside from the development of these part-time arrangements, the composition of the school has changed significantly as provision for children under seven has increased.

The school is run by staff committed to a behaviourist approach and has many distinctive features. There are two levels of structure provided for pupils. One is the organization of the day which is clearly divided into 'work' and 'reward' times. Pupils are made aware of exactly what is required of them and they are rewarded for appropriate behaviour. 'Tea and toast' sessions, for example, are available in the morning for children who have completed their assignments. There are also specific behavioural programmes designed for individual pupils. A system of tokens to reward acceptable behaviour operates throughout the school and a variety of 'treats' are available for purchase with these tokens. The school has a staff tutor who is responsible for providing courses for staff in relation to these structures and for organizing other in-service work and supervising newly-appointed staff.

The four nurture groups currently provide for up to 30 pupils between the ages of two and seven. All placements for two- to five-year-olds are part-time. Each group runs for two days of the week staffed by a teacher and a welfare assistant, with Wednesdays allocated for teachers to maintain links with the ordinary schools attended by their pupils. It is thought that one factor influencing the increasing number of young children attending the school is that people are aware that part-time attendance is available and that transfer to an ordinary school is a realistic option. On Wednesdays teachers may visit schools, make telephone contact with them, observe children in different settings, advise or guide the teachers taking these pupils or give instructions about specific programmes to be used for individual children.

The junior department can cater for 48 seven- to 11-year-olds. Of these, a third are full-time, a third attend mornings only and the rest come for only two afternoons a week. The majority of children in this department continue to attend their referring ordinary school, and Powell's Orchard teachers have time allotted to them to liaise with these schools. There are eight children in each group staffed by one teacher and one welfare assistant. In the morning sessions pupils cover academic work; in the afternoons the emphasis is on developing interpersonal relationships and engaging in leisure activities.

The secondary department caters for 24 full-time pupils, 16 attending mornings only, eight attending for four mornings and two afternoons, and 24 coming for up to three afternoon sessions. As with the junior age pupils, the morning and afternoon sessions are designed to serve different purposes. Secondary teachers with part-time pupils have one half day a week built into their timetable to work with ordinary schools. The emphasis here is on supporting pupils directly rather than working with other teachers.

Oakdale School

This is a school for pupils with severe learning difficulties located in a rural setting in a shire county. The school occupies a very attractive site with ample outdoor space and a range of facilities. There is a great deal of large play equipment available for the pupils.

Oakdale caters for pupils between the ages of two and 19. The 16–19 provision is for those who have a sensory impairment; other 16-year-olds can transfer to a unit in a nearby further education college for a two-year full-time course or to a hospital for a three-year part-time course. When initial visits were made for this research, only 35 of the 77 pupils on roll attended school on the main site. About 50 per cent of pupils were described as being profoundly handicapped by the headteacher who compared this to the average figure for a school such as this of 20–25 per cent. A small number of this group attend classes in units in nearby hospitals, but the majority of pupils are taught by teachers from the special school – in two adjacent schools, one primary and one secondary. The special school teachers have full responsibility for these pupils, who remain on the special school roll.

When the transfer of pupils to the primary school began in 1981, children were very carefully selected to participate because it was felt that they should be introduced gradually into other settings. This caution has become unnecessary as the contact with ordinary schools developed and children are now automatically sent to the nursery class at the primary school without selection. It is intended that children progress through this class to the infant and junior classes and then on to the secondary school. The nursery and infant accommodation is slightly separate from the main school building, although they are very much part of the school campus, and their large rooms have specialist equipment and changing facilities. The junior group are housed in an ordinary classroom without extra facilities or equipment. As the primary school links became established the headteacher of the comprehensive school was approached to discuss the possible placement of pupils who would otherwise have had to return to the main special school site, and the first pupils were introduced into secondary schooling in 1983. At the present time, pupils in the comprehensive school are accommodated in spare classrooms and it is envisaged that a purpose-built special care unit will be constructed on the campus to provide for the more severely handicapped pupils who will be attending as the scheme develops.

The pupils who attend ordinary schools still visit the special school for Friday afternoon assemblies and certain special occasions and festivals but they are very much part of the school they attend. They register at that school and are involved in assemblies and other whole-school events. Other pupils in the primary school come in pairs to the special classes to join in activities on a rota basis; in the secondary school pupils are allowed to stay indoors if they visit the special classes to mix with the pupils from Oakdale during the lunch break. Most of the Oakdale pupils in both schools eat in the main canteen. There are opportunities for social contact with other pupils during break times, and some Oakdale pupils regularly attend registration periods and classes in the ordinary school including metalwork, art and games. In the primary school pupils may join a class of juniors, taking their own work trays with them, and will then be involved in group activities such as watching television with the class. Where appropriate, individual children may spend up to a full day in a class with or without a welfare assistant. Oakdale staff consider the possibility of some sessions in ordinary classes when they review each pupil's progress. Although the teaching staff are working full-time in an ordinary school, they are members of the Oakdale staff and attend weekly curriculum meetings and fortnightly staff meetings at Oakdale.

The special school is situated a short drive away from the ordinary schools taking its pupils, and the movement of pupils does depend on efficient transport arrangements. Pupils may be transported by a member of staff or by one of the pool of volunteers who provide regular assistance. Physiotherapy is provided, as appropriate, by a therapist from the special school and there are regular visits from speech and music therapists.

Freelands School

Freelands School caters for 60 children with physical handicaps aged between two and 19. It shares a site with a first and middle school and a high school and is situated in an outer London borough. The school is organized into two sections with transfer at age 12. There is a considerable amount of both individual and group integration from Freelands, particularly for senior pupils, and some pupils from the ordinary schools spend time at Freelands on a regular basis. There are also staff exchanges in that teachers from Freelands are timetabled to work in the ordinary schools and vice versa. The close proximity of the schools has helped in building up the links between them.

The integration of senior pupils began in 1978 when two of them were introduced into classes at the high school. It has now grown to the extent that all but three of the 32 pupils over the age of 12 are included to varying degrees. Some of these pupils only attend for a short period of time, taking non-academic subjects, but more than half of them have a substantial commitment to examination courses in the high school. Twenty-one of the 32 are fully integrated except for games and heavy craft work. There is also some limited pupil movement in the other direction in that a group from the high school take a communications course in an integrated group at the special school.

Much of the high school is accessible and pupils who attend there generally travel the short distance involved unaided. Several of the seniors take trolleys with them to transport their computers and TV monitors. Support from a welfare assistant is available if required in lessons with a large practical component such as art and science. A toilet has been adapted at the high school for use by those in wheelchairs, and pupils are able to receive any practical assistance they need from welfare assistants based at the special school. Pupils from Freelands tend to gravitate back there at lunchtime where they can join in a variety of activities and meet up with their long-standing peers – it should be remembered that most have been part of the Freelands community for many years.

There are regular staff exchanges in that the deputy headteacher of Freelands teaches languages for three periods a week in the high school and one of the deputy heads from the high school spends the same amount of time teaching in Freelands. Two other teachers from Freelands take classes in the high school. In one instance, this involves team teaching remedial mathematics for four sessions a week where the aim is to pass on some of the special school knowledge and experience; the other teacher is involved in team teaching a lower sixth form group for literacy and communication.

Staff from the high school are encouraged to come and work in the junior groups in Freelands, particularly to provide practical curriculum advice and support. There is also contact between staff when pupils attend the first and middle school. Freelands teachers regularly teach in this ordinary school in classes allocated by the headteacher; one works there for half a morning a week in order to release a teacher to spend time in Freelands. Teachers take up this option in rotation.

It is hoped that this team teaching and exchange of staff will be extended in future years. The integration of the junior age children has only developed in the last two or three years and is mostly undertaken in the afternoons. The main exception is that on Friday mornings all Freelands children go across, as a group, for assembly in the ordinary school and stay for the rest of the morning doing activities of various kinds. A small number of children are involved on an individual basis, but most attend as a group. There is a joint music and drama session in Freelands each week when pupils come over from the ordinary school. Children from the ordinary school's nursery regularly use Freelands' swimming pool and a small number of junior age pupils have come for core curriculum work in the mornings. A welfare assistant is always present in the ordinary school when children from Freelands attend. As the schools are so close together, arranging for physiotherapy is reasonably straightforward. Any of the senior pupils who need this support are given priority and it is fitted around their timetable. It is the younger children who receive the most intensive help and they are all on the special school site for much of their time.

The Priory School

This school caters for children with emotional, behavioural and learning problems who are characterized by having had a 'breakdown in management' of one sort or another. There are 56 such children on the roll. The school officially takes pupils from the age of five, but most are aged at least eight years when they arrive and have experienced great difficulty in the schools they have attended. Some travel a considerable distance to the school as pupils are accepted from all parts of the shire county in which the school is located. Pupils usually remain in the school for between two and five years, with a minimum stay of about 18 months. There is a commitment on the part of the staff at The Priory to return pupils to ordinary schools by the age of 11, where possible. Another special school in the area caters for pupils of 13 years and upwards who are not considered suitable for placement in ordinary schools.

The pupils vary considerably in their needs and, while there is an overall staff–pupil ratio of one to seven, the actual size of classes varies from three to 11. The school is grouped into three mixed-age bands, according to the severity of their problems. Band 1 contains pupils with the most severe problems and has the most favourable staff–pupil ratio, while Band 3 contains pupils who are being considered for an ordinary school placement. While ordinary school placements are introduced on a gradual basis, it is always the intention that pupils transfer full-time to the ordinary school roll. This places a premium on the careful selection of pupils for placement and on close monitoring of their progress in the ordinary school. A classroom assistant is attached to each band and they are able to provide support in other schools if it is thought appropriate.

The deputy headteacher records that in the last few years 18 out of a potential 29 pupils have been placed in ordinary schools, all except two returning to schools in their own locality. Only one pupil has been re-referred. The staff emphasize that the success of the scheme depends on the considerable groundwork that they undertake. The pupils attending ordinary schools for part of the week are widely dispersed so that making contact with relevant staff and visiting pupils in class requires careful planning. The support provided by Priory staff varies depending on what each pupil or the staff in their receiving school are thought to need. The aim for many pupils is to guide them through a crisis period and then to facilitate their placement in another school.

Pupils have usually come from a primary school and are entering a secondary setting, so that it would be unusual for them to be returning to the same school. The idea of transfer is presented to pupils in a very positive light and the curriculum is planned to run on parallel with what they might be doing in their other classes. Moving to an ordinary school is regarded as the next logical step for pupils who have made progress at The Priory. Pupils initially attend the mainstream school for one day a week. Their placement is monitored and is the subject of a review meeting held at The Priory. Their time in the ordinary school is gradually extended, depending on progress, until a full-time placement is made.

Two teachers are specifically involved in 'servicing' the pupils attending ordinary schools; for one, this forms a substantial commitment, involving most of her timetable. While there is contact with ordinary school teachers concerning the progress of individual pupils, the visits are primarily viewed as offering emotional and practical support to the pupils involved. All of those placed in ordinary classes are seen regularly but the duration and frequency of the visits made by the support teacher are determined on an individual basis. The teacher's role with the class also varies depending on the needs of the pupil involved and the content of the lessons visited. Support teachers may work directly with one pupil or confine themselves to observing the classroom experience of that pupil, or they may team teach or work with the whole group.

Standlake School

This is an all-age special school for pupils with physical handicaps, having nearly 100 pupils on roll. There is some residential accommodation available on site as pupils may travel a considerable distance to attend the school, situated as it is in a large shire county. Standlake is staffed by 17 teachers including the headteacher and 14 classroom assistants. There are full-time and part-time physiotherapists, care staff and nurses. Standlake School shares a campus with Greenfields Comprehensive School with which a link involving the movement of pupils has been established. At the time of this research there were 13 pupils going across to fourth year classes (one of whom is full-time on an O-level course), one full-time second year pupil and six pupils attending sixth form classes. There were eight pupils spending more than ten hours a week in the comprehensive school, and the range of time spent in these classes varied from two to 29 hours. There are currently few links with the primary schools in the locality so pupils may experience their first contact with an ordinary school when they go to Greenfields.

The trend is for Standlake to take pupils who are more severely handicapped and who have learning difficulties as well as physical limitations. Staff at the school do not envisage any increase in the number of pupils spending time in Greenfields and assume that it will be a fairly steady proportion of their roll. Pupils are carefully considered in terms of their ability to benefit from some experience in an ordinary school when their placement is under review. Age is not a crucial factor although, on the whole, pupils attend Greenfields from their fourth year when curriculum options are being considered. Staff at Standlake have suggested that, because the first three years of secondary schooling are so vital in terms of developing basic academic skills, they prefer to consolidate those themselves for pupils who are experiencing difficulty. It is felt that there are pupils who would benefit from the social contact and stimulation but would be unable to cope emotionally with attending an ordinary school. There could be occasions when a whole group of pupils could usefully go across together as the link develops.

The headteacher feels that it is in the social sphere that they 'expect and gain most of the successes' but that the educational gains are becoming more apparent as pupils obtain access to certain subjects and examinations. Pupils attend for a variety of subjects including child care, art, typing, biology and computer studies. There have been recent examination successes in English, computer studies and economics. One pupil attends the sixth form on a full-time basis, returning to Standlake for lunch and over night accommodation. She was referred to Standlake from a school where her disability was seen as problematic. The full-time second year pupil has been attending on this basis from the age of 11. She returns to the special school for physiotherapy and to use the pool, and is thought to derive practical and emotional support from her contact with those at the special school. The full-time O-level pupil is said to have a 'strong link' with the special school and frequently goes there at the start of the day and to eat her lunch in their dining room.

The two schools are divided by a large playing field and the path to be crossed, while not very long, is extremely exposed. Some pupils with very restricted mobility can travel in motorized scooters supplied from the special school. In other instances a pupil in a wheelchair will be pushed by a more mobile peer or aided by a friend in an electric wheelchair. Pupils are sometimes accompanied across the field by a classroom assistant if required; they may need help with transporting equipment of some sort. A full-time classroom assistant has recently been appointed at Greenfields, partly to assist the physically handicapped pupils in their classes. She will be available to assist them as they travel across the site, to provide practical help in the lessons and to deal with any issues arising from their time spent in Greenfields. Ramps have been laid at Greenfields to aid mobility, toilets have been adapted, and lifts have been installed to enable all pupils from Standlake to move freely around the building.

Larkshill School

This all-age special school in a northern county caters for pupils with a range of learning difficulties. There are 135 children on roll and until recently the school was divided into two separate establishments – one for children with moderate learning difficulties and another for those with severe learning difficulties, including those requiring special care. The integration of these two establishments is seen as part of a climate that has led to the development of links with one primary and two comprehensive schools. The link principally involves the movement of pupils with moderate learning difficulties from Larkshill to the three ordinary schools. Two teachers from Larkshill are also involved in the other schools. The link is essentially one-way although some pupils do visit to use its pool and gymnasium.

The links began when the headteacher of a local primary school approached Larkshill for advice about dealing with some less able children. This contact prompted Larkshill's headteacher to inquire about linking with local secondary schools. Two headteachers expressed interest, and the four heads met to organize possible strategies. The first link involved nine third and fourth year juniors moving with their teacher to the primary school to form a 'satellite' class. Of these nine, two are still attending the primary school, six have moved on to one of the comprehensive schools and one has returned to Larkshill. The two still at the school are fully integrated into fourth year groups. At the time of the research there were six children from Larkshill forming a 'satellite' class with their teacher. As soon as they attend the primary school they are involved in a variety of activities including physical education, music, art and assembly, only returning to their home base for academic work. The aim is to introduce them gradually to their new school, with a view to full transfer eventually. They remain on the special school roll.

The teacher responsible for the satellite class works full-time at the primary school although he is a member of Larkshill staff. He works primarily with the children from Larkshill but his role changes as the children are absorbed into classes. His mornings are spent team teaching with a primary school teacher in a group of top infants and first year juniors; in the afternoons he undertakes remedial work in a variety of settings. This involves withdrawing children from their normal classes or working with teachers in their classes if that seems appropriate. The children transferring from Larkshill are candidates for this extra work, but they are taught in groups alongside their primary school peers.

The links with the two comprehensive schools are rather different.

One of these schools agreed to take 14- and 15-year-old pupils to provide them with some experience in an integrated setting before they left school; the other provides for those pupils who are ready to transfer from the primary school. There were three pupils taking advantage of the first option in Atwood School at the time of this research. Pupils at the secondary stage attend ordinary schools on a full-time integrated basis, although they are withdrawn for some sessions with the support teacher from Larkshill. The three pupils at Atwood all attended ordinary primary schools until their middle junior years when they were referred to Larkshill. They have two sessions during the week when they work in a small group with the support teacher; otherwise they are simply in ordinary classes or are taught by the support teacher as members of a larger group. The six pupils who have moved on to Berkeley School are similarly placed in that they integrate fully but receive regular support from the Larkshill teacher.

The Larkshill teacher involved in the secondary level links divides most of her working week between the two comprehensive schools. Her brief is to work with the transferred pupils as well as other pupils with learning difficulties and to take a pastoral interest in the Larkshill pupils. During her two days in Atwood she teaches groups containing only pupils from Larkshill, 'mixed' groups and some with only Atwood pupils. In her two days at Berkeley School she works mainly on a withdrawal basis with the Larkshill pupils who have transferred from the primary school, although she also assists with mixed ability science lessons. As more pupils transfer to this school via the primary school scheme described above, there will be more demands made on the support teacher's time and a full-time appointment is likely to be required.

Elm Grange School

This school for pupils with moderate learning difficulties is involved in links with one infant and three primary schools. The Elm Grange Support Service includes a resource centre at the school that is available to mainstream teachers in the area, but the main function of the link is for Elm Grange teachers to teach pupils of primary age in the ordinary schools using packs of individually prepared structured learning materials. There are 135 pupils on the school roll but this number is decreasing as fewer pupils are referred. The scheme was established nearly eight years ago and extra teaching staff were allocated to it from the authority. The support teachers aim to provide advice about the assessment and selection of pupils but the ordinary schools decide which pupils are withdrawn. Help is available for up to 12 children, who would normally be top infants and first year juniors from each of the four schools. The service is designed to be flexible so that it can respond to whatever requests individual 'consumers' make.

Support is available in a variety of curriculum areas. The predominant arrangement is that pupils are withdrawn from their classes for individual sessions of about 20 minutes duration. This time is used to discuss the pupils' progress through their work pack, to teach the next stage to be covered and to set work for completion during the following week in school. Two teachers from Elm Grange are attached to one school where they undertake this work together on one morning each week. Their afternoons are spent working through the assignments completed by the pupils they are supporting and preparing the new materials that are central to the development of the service.

These arrangements require collaboration and consultation between Elm Grange teachers and the ordinary school staff as the former are essentially leaving work for the latter to supervise during the coming week. In some instances this consultation has led to pupils being allocated a place in Elm Grange. The service may change in emphasis if collaborating with staff means that their requests are met. One headteacher, for example, would like to work towards a situation where Elm Grange teachers are working as part of a team within the classrooms and provide in-service training in relation to less able pupils. In one instance a teacher from Elm Grange works in a class, specifically to help a child who has a very poor concept of number. She spends time with the pupil alone, with a small group containing this pupil and with the teacher who values the guidance she has to offer about other pupils whose development is of concern. She provides worksheets for use with other pupils in the class, as appropriate. In another school, contact with Elm Grange staff is seen as a way of 'easing the passage of pupils' into the special school. Children work through their assignments during the week and are withdrawn to discuss their progress. In the year previous to the research three of them had transferred to Elm Grange.

Elm Grange shares a site with a school catering for secondary age pupils with moderate learning difficulties that has links of a rather different kind with ordinary schools. Three of their teachers are currently working with teachers in three comprehensive schools. An extra 0.5 of a member of teaching staff has been allocated to the school to facilitate this arrangement. The work undertaken in ordinary schools has varied considerably. One teacher, for example, spent half a day every fortnight in one school for a period of two terms, planning a programme of work for less able pupils doing needlework. She passed on her methods and examples of work to the teacher in the ordinary school for the latter's use. One of the schools currently involved receives two visits from special school staff each week and the others one visit each. The teachers have been involved in this team work in English, mathematics, needlework and home economics.

In one school two special school teachers currently spend one afternoon a week in the remedial department. They are concerned with both mathematics and English and have provided worksheets and advice on grouping pupils and teaching techniques. In another case a teacher visits a comprehensive school for an afternoon each week to join in teaching a group of 13 pupils for home economics. Again it is intended to provide worksheets and give practical advice about teaching strategies.

Ashdown School

This school was opened on a campus site between an 11–16 comprehensive school and a primary school. Integration at the primary stage was initiated nearly eight years ago and involved pupils spending part of their time in the ordinary school from the first or second year junior stage and then moving on to the comprehensive school for a proportion of their work. The primary school has now closed and plans are being formulated to develop links with another primary school about a quarter of a mile from Ashdown and to encourage the placement of more physically handicapped pupils in their local schools.

At the secondary level, there are substantial links with the on-site comprehensive school. These had led to plans being formulated and approved by the local education authority, which will, in the near future, result in the transfer of all senior pupils into purpose-built accommodation in the comprehensive school. At the time of this research, 24 out of the 45 secondary age pupils from Ashdown were spending varying amounts of time ranging from four lessons a week to 75 per cent of their timetable in the secondary school. In addition, several pupils who spent more than 75 per cent of their time in the comprehensive school had been transferred to the roll of that school, and only attended Ashdown for physiotherapy or medical treatment.

Ashdown is to become a primary school, and a nursery assessment unit for physically handicapped pupils, currently based in a local hospital, will transfer there.

Pupils integrating into the secondary school do so for the full range of subject options. Where there is a question over the amount of integration that pupils can cope with, account is taken of their individual strengths and weaknesses and personal preferences. However, since Ashdown cannot offer the full range of options, special consideration is given to early integration into subject areas which could be difficult to pick up later, such as modern languages; and subjects such as mathematics and English, which are adequately covered at Ashdown, are frequently added to the integration programme at a later stage. Pupils were initially selected to join mainstream classes on the basis of academic ability, but, more recently, less able pupils have been included. One complication of this very flexible form of integration has been the difficulty in maintaining a balanced curriculum for pupils who spend time in both the comprehensive school and Ashdown, and this was one of the factors which led to the plans for the transfer of secondary age pupils being formulated.

The comprehensive school has been allocated three extra teachers to allow them to accommodate the physically handicapped pupils already attending. This extra staffing is used to reduce overall pupil–teacher ratios. In addition, teachers from Ashdown are available to provide advice and information about pupils as appropriate. Ancillary help is also available from Ashdown for certain practical subjects.

When the transfer of secondary pupils from Ashdown takes place, a new department catering for all pupils with special needs will be set up within the comprehensive school. This will be staffed by eight teachers including the head of department. Some staff from Ashdown will transfer, and the additional three teachers at present allocated to the comprehensive school will be included in the eight teaching staff. The head of department, who has been appointed at Senior Teacher level and was previously second deputy at Ashdown, has been appointed a year in advance of the planned transfer in order to engage in detailed planning and to collaborate with other heads of departments. An initial financial allowance has been made, and the purchase of appropriate equipment is proceeding. It is intended that there will be integration of staff as well as pupils between the Special Needs and other departments so that Special Needs staff will spend part of their time teaching mainstream pupils and vice versa. The Special Needs staff will also provide support to colleagues whose classes include pupils with special needs, as well as teaching these pupils within the Special Needs department.

Fyfield House

Fyfield House is a school providing secondary education for hearing impaired pupils. Some pupils attending the school come from outside the shire county in which it is situated and residential accommodation is available. The 28 pupils on roll now spend so much of their time in the nearby comprehensive school that Fyfield House is being 'absorbed' into it. The schools in question are separated by playing fields that may be crossed by a ten minute walk. Most pupils referred to the school have severely impaired hearing. When the school was opened about ten years ago it was intended that it would provide specialist help to hearing impaired pupils who would receive most of their education in classes in the nearby comprehensive school. The school building was designed with this goal in mind and consists of a series of small, separate units. However, the school did function for several years as the teaching base for its pupils and it is only fairly recently that the original plan has been followed through. The school building will house a resource centre for those working with hearing impaired pupils and will be used as a base for a variety of activities by staff and pupils. It is used, for example, for sixth form art classes.

When the links began, pupils from Fyfield House attended the ordinary school for a few sessions in practical subjects with most of their academic work being covered at Fyfield House. The move towards full integration began two years ago and has been monitored by a panel concerned with special needs provision in the authority. Six teachers, originally from Fyfield House, support pupils in classes, i.e. one for each year group. An art and craft teacher provides part-time support for some groups containing hearing impaired pupils.

In their first two years in the comprehensive school all hearing impaired pupils are in the same group with the school and after that they are dispersed into different groups as they choose from the subject options available. Pupils from Fyfield House are involved in all aspects of school life. Rooms are available in the ordinary school for hearing impaired pupils to be withdrawn for individual sessions although use of this facility is kept to an absolute minimum.

The main support provided by Fyfield House teachers is within the classroom where pupils' participation in lessons is carefully monitored. The support teachers and their colleagues in ordinary schools aim to work as a team and share responsibility for the whole group of pupils as appropriate. Equipment such as phonic ears and radio microphones is available and utilized throughout the school. When they are withdrawn from classes pupils are given extra English work, speech therapy and any support in other subjects that they may require. Those who are boarding may have some tuition during the evening and after school.

4 Establishing and Developing Link Schemes

Link arrangements involve local education authorities and schools in quite different ways. This is particularly evident in the setting up of schemes. This chapter traces the reasons at authority and school level why link schemes were set up, finding in each case a mixture of opportunism and concern for children's education. The authority's involvement in setting up schemes ranges from reacting to initiatives taken by individual schools to taking the lead itself and exercising close control over developments. The school's role in establishing link schemes is considered in terms of selecting partner schools and identifying pupils to participate. Finally, some issues relating to the continuing development of link arrangements are noted.

LEA perspective

Who is the LEA?

There is a problem when referring to the 'LEA' in determining exactly what is meant and which people in particular are being referred to. This is discussed in detail in the accompanying volume on local authority support services (Moses *et al.*, 1988). Here it is necessary to clarify who is likely to be responsible at local authority level for the different aspects of link schemes.

The extent of the scheme is an important factor here. Where there are major resource implications or substantial issues of policy, senior officers and possibly elected members will be involved. Examples would be where link schemes develop to the point where new posts need to be established or major building works are required. In some cases link schemes may involve so many pupils spending so much of their time in the ordinary school that the future of the special school is called into question. Again, this is a circumstance that may well involve decisions by the elected members.

The more substantial link schemes can be seen as a type of organization or reorganization forming one aspect of an authority's provision that furthers a policy of providing for pupils with a wide range of special needs in ordinary schools. In these situations advisers and education officers will commonly be involved. Elected members would not usually be involved at this level.

When the authority was involved in the link schemes studied, the leading role was taken by special needs staff – the adviser for special education and the assistant education officer for special education. The main significance of this is that, although links involve both the special and ordinary sectors of education, they are seen as more centrally the concern of the special sector and most of them originate from the special schools. While links involve the movement of staff, pupils and resources in both directions, both from and to special schools, the most significant movement is from special schools to ordinary schools. Such link schemes are likely to have more of an impact on the special schools than on the ordinary schools.

Phase advisers, subject advisers and psychologists could be involved in the development of link schemes, but none of the case study schemes was characterized by their active, long-term involvement. It is becoming common that advisers for special education have included in their job description the giving of advice in a general way to ordinary schools and/or responsibility for advising on special educational needs in ordinary schools. Where this is the case, the adviser for special education is in a particularly favourable position from which to contribute to link schemes.

Why links?

Link schemes have developed for a variety of reasons, at both authority and school levels. Two types of consideration may be discerned where the authority is the instigator: one, where links emerge essentially in response to falling school rolls and one where links are positively sought in their own right and planned as an integral feature of an authority's entire special needs provision. The schools studied in this research catered for children with a wide variety of special needs, and this was reflected in the differing rationales and aims of the link schemes that were established.

It is of considerable significance that links between ordinary and special schools are being established at a time of falling school rolls. The proportion of children in special schools has, at least until recently, been relatively constant since the early seventies (Hegarty *et al.*, 1981), though some categories of special school, e.g. those catering for primary age children with moderate learning difficulties, have seen an increase (Swann, 1985). At the same time the overall number of school-age children has been declining so that the actual number of children in special schools has decreased, even if not as dramatically as in some ordinary primary schools.

In the special schools, falling rolls have frequently led to the situation where the teacher/pupil ratio is considerably more favourable than that recommended by the Department of Education and Science's staffing guidelines. These are the circumstances that can lead to schools losing staff and with them their particular expertise. Compared with ordinary schools, special schools tend to have fewer pupils and staff, so that the loss of a member of staff when the school roll is falling may well leave the school without a particular expertise and the pupils deprived of a specialist to teach subjects such as music, maths, science and PE. Rather than allow this to happen, some authorities have maintained staffing levels at special schools by giving teachers a range of additional functions, such as those involved in establishing a link scheme or a resource centre.

Rolls are also falling in ordinary schools, with the result that staff there are similarly available for redeployment. Again, one of the ways in which this can be achieved is by involving staff in a link scheme. Falling rolls lead to surplus accommodation and, in extreme cases, to the threat of school closure. Link schemes provide a means of making appropriate use of spare space and of staving off politically unpopular and administratively difficult school closures. It is worth noting that falling rolls make it easier to set up links from the ordinary schools' perspective. They may be more willing, as well as possibly more able, to take pupils with special needs when their numbers are falling. When schools were still expanding and accommodation often restricted it would have been much more difficult to organize such schemes.

It must not be supposed that local education authorities only embark on link schemes when forced to do so by pressure of falling rolls and the need to deploy teachers. There are some positive reasons as well. At least three situations can be identified where links are sought as valuable in their own right: establishing resource centres;

implementing the Education Act 1981; and formulating authority-wide policies.

Some authorities have identified a need for resource centres in special education. These are centres where up-to-date information is kept on curriculum materials, teaching and assessment approaches, and good practice in special education generally; they may also provide in-service training as well as advice to individual teachers and schools. In many cases it was agreed that the most appropriate way of establishing such a special centre was to build it on the base of a special school.

Implementing the 1981 Act gives education authorities a further reason for adopting link schemes. In particular, there is the pressing problem of enabling ordinary schools to fulfil their obligations under the Act in assessing their pupils' special needs, providing from their own resources for most of these pupils and securing the 'extra' resources required for pupils for whom Statements are written. Although all authorities run some support services to assist individual pupils with special needs and their teachers in ordinary schools, virtually all are very hard pressed and would benefit from more assistance. In these circumstances, many authorities see the establishment of links with special schools as going at least part of the way to alleviate this problem.

Finally, some authorities have adopted formal policy documents outlining their special needs provision. Typically, these lay down guiding principles, detail the different forms of provision available within the authority, specify relevant procedures and note significant developments for the future. Such policy documents can incorporate link schemes and ensure that they have a coherent and planned place within the range of provision for special needs in the authority.

Nature of LEA involvement

Link schemes mark a significant departure in educational provision. They embody some unusual practices: teachers working in schools other than the one to which they are appointed and outside the jurisdiction of the headteacher to whom they are responsible; pupils attending two schools or attending one school while being on the roll of another; and resources acquired by one school being used principally in another school. Given all of this, local authorities have to become involved – the administrative and other implications are such that link schemes cannot remain at the sole discretion of the participating schools.

As with virtually all aspects of educational provision, there is considerable variation between and within authorities. Our data would suggest four stances that an authority can take, in that they can:

1 react to individual school schemes
2 exert indirect influence
3 set a general direction but leave individual schools to determine details
4 exercise close control.

These are not sharply divided categories and may overlap in practice. Moreover, an individual authority is likely to operate flexibly and modify its stance in accordance with the type of school involved and the nature of the link scheme. Particularly in larger authorities with an area management structure, there may be systematic variation between the different parts of the authority – close control in one area and indirect influence elsewhere for example.

Reacting to individual school schemes

Many link schemes are set up as the result of initiatives by individual headteachers and schools. As we shall see later in the chapter, these initiatives can be taken for a variety of reasons, ranging from fears about survival to an ideological commitment to integration. Whatever the motivation, it must be realized that individual schools enjoy consider-able autonomy and when they choose to exercise it in this way the authority is cast into a reacting role.

If more than a minimum of activity is involved in a link scheme the authority will have to be made aware of it. It will have to give at least tacit permission for staff and pupils to spend parts of the school week away from their own schools. It will also have to react to the inevitable resourcing implications. In the normal course of events, schools are budgeted for as single, self-contained units, and resources, especially teachers, are allocated to them on the basis of pupil numbers. The allocations are not generally such as to allow the luxury of working with other pupils not on the school roll. At the very least, the authority would have to approve the transfer of resources from one school to another and they may need to intervene actively to facilitate the transfer. It is more likely, however, since the necessary resources cannot be parcelled up for exact transfers, that some extra resources will be required: actually running a complex link scheme may call for an additional teacher, items of equipment may need to be duplicated to save continually ferrying them from school to school, additional transport arrangements may be necessary for children attending two schools. The authority must then respond to the case for extra resources and provide them as it sees fit.

There are a number of pitfalls for a special school which attempts to offer support to ordinary schools without the knowledge and positive backing of the authority. Although such schemes can be started, there are inevitable problems in sustaining them.

    i   Children in special schools are the subject of Statements. The authority is directly responsible for 'extra' educational provision for these children and is therefore responsible for what they may require when in ordinary schools. If it does not endorse their presence in an ordinary school or does not even know about it, it can hardly be said to be carrying out its statutory duties.

    ii   Schools are budgeted for and staffed as single units, and it is only when they are 'over-staffed' that teachers can legitimately spend time anywhere other than in their own school. This 'over-staffing' has to be approved by the authority if it is to be anything other than temporary. If teachers from special schools that are not over-staffed spend a substantial amount of their working week in other schools, it inevitably results in less favourable staff/pupil ratios at the special school. This again may affect the quality of education on offer and is the responsibility of the authority.

    iii   There are problems of replicating services, possibly leading to confusion and even conflict. Ordinary schools can be supported by the school psychological service, the remedial or other support services and by the special school. It would be possible for a pupil and his or her teacher to receive support from each of these sources quite independently of the others. At best this is a replication of service that probably means too much help is going in one direction and not enough in another; at worst it can result in conflicting advice and support of incompatible kinds being offered.

One of the first of the support services organized independently by the headteacher of a school for pupils with moderate learning difficulties found itself very unpopular in the authority for these reasons. Ordinary schools complained to the authority about the conflicting advice they were receiving from the special school teachers and staff from the remedial service, while the latter felt that their work in schools was being undermined. In the event, the officer in charge of special education reacted by stopping the scheme. He was able to do this by not renewing the contracts of staff in temporary posts; this effectively reduced the school's staffing level so that all staff were required for pupils in the special school itself. The surplus of materials and equipment that the school had acquired to assist staff working in ordinary schools was also withdrawn and relocated in a neighbouring primary school where a new special needs support service was established.

Exercising indirect influence

Moving on from merely reacting to school initiatives, authorities can exercise a good deal of indirect influence in the setting up of link schemes. This is most evident in two areas, viz the making of new appointments and the siting of new schools.

Authorities' control over appointments is a major factor in policy implementation, stretching far beyond link schemes. If an authority wishes to implement a new policy and the preference is for indirect influence rather than overt direction, it may decide to further the policy through appointing people with particular views. A key position in this respect is that of the headteacher. Although headteachers are employed by and are directly responsible to the authority, they exercise considerable autonomy and are powerfully placed to advance – or hinder – the implementation of given policies.

Thus, an authority can further a policy of link schemes by appointing to headships staff who are committed to such links. Indeed, in some cases, authorities see themselves as having originated schemes through appointing staff who were known to be committed to the idea of links and ensuring that, despite falling rolls, the special school retained its former level of staffing. The daily running of the scheme is left in the hands of the head but the authority can still exert a good deal of influence on its development through the advisory service and possibly the school psychological service.

The schools may of course view the situation in a very different light. A newly appointed headteacher who establishes a link scheme is likely to regard it as his or her own idea. The location of the school in relation to other schools is likely to be viewed as fortuitous as much as anything else. Similarly, the level of staffing may be viewed differently from the way the authority sees it. The head may feel that he or she has a certain number of teachers with which to staff the school. If teachers start to spend a substantial part of their timetable in other schools then it could appear that more teachers are necessary; ancillary staff may be regarded in the same way.

Headteachers of ordinary schools may interpret the situation in much the same way, particularly when the link scheme involves pupils from the special school spending time in the ordinary school. No matter what the class size or staffing levels in the school, the addition of pupils with special needs is almost certainly going to be regarded as an 'extra' commitment and responsibility at the school. This school may well feel that extra staffing and possibly extra equipment and materials are needed. The authority may be providing extra transport but, from the perspective of the ordinary school, this is likely to go unnoticed. There are many instances where an ordinary school has been allocated an extra assistant mainly because of the presence of pupils who have come into the school on link schemes. However, the school is likely to take the view that this assistance was needed in any case and it may well have been trying to secure this appointment prior to the establishment of the link. The authority considers that more resources have been provided but the school does not.

The different perspectives of local authority and school(s) are well illustrated by the Larkshill scheme. The arrangement was for the eight children to form a 'satellite' class, taking with them a teacher from the special school who, in the first instance, taught the class of eight children for most of the time. When the children were in ordinary classes their teacher was freed for remedial work with other children. As the members of the satellite class gradually dispersed into the ordinary school, their teacher became increasingly available for other duties in the school. The numbers in the special school were such that it was becoming increasingly difficult to justify the level of staffing, and it would have been impossible for the school to lose eight children and not lose a teacher. When the eight children moved into the ordinary school, taking a full-time member of the teaching staff with them, the primary school gained an extra teacher but only eight additional pupils.

The heads of the two schools also arranged other contact between the schools; pupils from the special school attended music sessions in the primary school and classes from the primary school went to the special school to use their very good sports facilities. In these circumstances the authority regarded the link as well resourced but the headteachers felt otherwise. They both argued that the activities of both their schools had been expanded but no new resources had been found for them. The heads knew that they had the backing of the authority, in the form of the approval of the officer and adviser responsible for special education, but felt let down as far as resources were concerned.

A second way in which local authorities can exercise indirect influence is in the siting of new school buildings. This is an infrequent opportunity of course, but when it occurs the authority can elect to build a new special school close by an existing primary or secondary school. In some cases it has been possible to have a comprehensive, primary and special school all on the same campus. Various other factors can be at work here. It may simply be that the particular site is the best available one within the neighbourhood and is large enough for several schools. When link schemes do become established between schools on a shared campus however, it is not unusual for the authority to claim that this very development had been the intention all along and that it had simply waited for this to come about naturally within the framework it had established. As with appointments, schools and headteachers may view the authority's role quite differently and be quite convinced that any links developed are entirely of their doing.

Giving a general direction

Another stance which the authority can take is to declare itself in favour of certain developments or to advocate certain policy directions without making them mandatory. It can set out a general policy for future developments while leaving the details to be settled by individual schools. Where link schemes are concerned, this would be in addition to exercising indirect influence of the type just described and would certainly entail reacting to the initiatives of individual schools.

This approach is exemplified by a shire county authority which adopted a policy designed to encourage link schemes but leaving schools free to develop the schemes they considered best suited to their individual circumstances and the needs of the neighbouring schools. The advisory team for special education requested each special school in the authority to draw up plans describing how they could promote contact with other schools. The schemes should have long-term aims of the placement of as many pupils as possible back in ordinary schools and high levels of provision for all pupils with special educational needs. Within this very wide brief special schools were free to devise their plans which could involve the movement of staff, pupils and resources in both directions, in and out of the special school. The special schools all submitted schemes. (It is perhaps significant that none decided not to participate, though the schemes drawn up by some were much more extensive than those drawn up by others.) In 1983 the authority produced a booklet which contained the plans of all the special schools in the authority. The exercise made the special schools consider their future and the range of new activities they could be involved in. The actual production of the booklet formalized the authority's stance over this issue and made the intentions of each school public knowledge.

Within this framework of policy direction and encouragement, the authority reacts to the individual initiatives of schools. The advantage for schools from the authority declaring its support for link schemes lies in the commitment made by the authority to try to make the schemes work. Furthering link schemes is a public objective of the authority, and schools involved in this activity can expect to have the backing of the authority, both morally and in resource terms.

Exercising close control

Close control by the authority can be exercised in relation to one particular scheme or, less usually, over a unified system of support. The relative autonomy granted to schools and the diversity of policy and practice in most areas of education make it unlikely that authorities that do not exercise close control in other areas of provision are going to single out link schemes for special consideration. However, in authorities that have a history of greater direction from the Education Office, close control of link schemes is possible and can be seen to have certain advantages.

These advantages are most clearly seen in relation to the allocation of resources in the instances where pupils attend more than one school on a regular basis and in the organizing of support for pupils and teachers in ordinary schools. There are many potential pitfalls for the special school that offers support to the ordinary school, with uncoordinated activity resulting in the replication and uneven distribution of support. A policy of close control can go a long way towards overcoming these problems.

It is possible for the help offered by the special schools to form part of the assistance offered by the whole range of support services. An example of this practice in action is provided by a metropolitan authority with a history of strong central direction. Each primary school in the authority is regarded as being in the 'catchment' area of one of the three special schools for pupils with moderate learning difficulties. As part of the routine work of the special needs support team, a member of this team may suggest that contact with the special school would be useful in assisting the primary school to solve a particular problem, either in relation to an individual child or an area of provision in the school. A contract stating the exact nature of the assistance to be offered, for what purpose and over what period of time, is drawn up by the head of the support team and agreed to by the participating schools. Replication of support is avoided in this way and all the special and ordinary schools are included in the same organizational framework.

It is also possible for an authority to exercise considerable influence over a more limited number of initiatives without incorporating them into an authority-wide, unified system. The process of close control can be viewed as an extension of the type of activity which may well have originated as exerting indirect influence. For example, a shire county which was an innovator in this field built a new special school and appointed staff specifically with the intention that the school should offer support to neighbouring primary schools. The direct involvement of the authority did not cease with the establishment of the scheme but continued through the school psychological service and the advisory service.

School perspective

Why links?

We saw above that link schemes became established at authority level because of two contrasting sets of reasons; the pressures and opportunities created by falling rolls and the intention of improving educational provision for pupils with special needs by incorporating the different aspects of provision into a coherent plan. A similar pattern of causation can be detected at the school level. Falling rolls and all the threats to survival that they represent are certainly a potent factor, but there are other reasons, too, that are rooted in concern for children's educational benefit. Apart from being significant in their own right, these more positive considerations are important for giving the lie to some sociologists of education who view special education in a naive, unidimensional way and regard any changes as designed primarily to serve the interests of the professionals involved.

Some of the early schemes were established by special school headteachers who felt that their schools were being seriously threatened by the recommendations of the Warnock Report, and it is easy to understand these fears. Although the Report emphasized that there would be special schools into the foreseeable future, the emphasis was on pupils with multiple and severe disabilities remaining in special schools while many others would transfer to ordinary schools. Special schools for pupils with moderate learning difficulties felt particularly vulnerable for they feared that if integration policies were really going to be implemented their pupils would be in the vanguard. The position of those pupils with learning difficulties and those with behaviour problems was seen as quite different in nature from that of those with other handicapping conditions. In particular, it was intimately connected with available levels of educational provision. In fact, provision varied greatly from one authority to another and the type of schooling a pupil received depended just as much on the receptiveness of the local primary and secondary schools and the availability of special school places as it did on the characteristics and needs of the pupil. Research demonstrated – what common experience had long suspected – that pupils with a particular pattern of difficulties attending a special school would, if they lived elsewhere, be receiving an adequate education in an ordinary school (cf. Hegarty *et al.*, 1981). It is easy to see how, in these circumstances, many special schools did not feel confident about the future and saw a possible salvation in the development of link schemes.

Special schools have not been motivated only by fears about survival, however. Some saw link schemes as a positive opportunity to demonstrate their expertise and, more importantly, to make it more widely available. A further recommendation of the Warnock Report, as described in Chapter 1 of this book, was that some special schools should be designated and developed as resource centres and should become centres of specialist expertise. This recommendation did have its threatening aspects – if special schools were to be regarded as centres of expertise they would have to display their skills in public and be much more open to scrutiny than in the past – but it had very real attractions to the heads of some special schools who had confidence in what their schools could offer and the energy and enthusiasm to expand their work. It gave them the chance not only to show the rest of the educational world what they could do but also to make their expertise available to other pupils who might benefit from it. Schemes that originate in this way are most likely to involve the movement of teachers out into ordinary schools to offer support and can be regarded as expansionist in nature.

A further motivation for link schemes is the belief that they enhance the education of particular pupils. This belief underpins those schemes that involve the movement of pupils out into ordinary schools. Such schemes reduce the amount of teaching done in the special school, they reduce the time pupils spend in special schools and they are likely to reduce the actual number of pupils. Frequently, the aim is to maximize the amount of time that pupils spend in ordinary schools but to do so gradually and flexibly. The link is seen as a progressive series of steps leading ultimately to a full-time, permanent placement in the ordinary school.

One of the outstanding characteristics of many of the schemes is their dynamic nature. Link schemes cannot be regarded as a type of provision that, once established, will necessarily continue in a close approximation of its original form. During the course of the research three schools have been observed taking irrevocable steps towards total absorption by the ordinary schools to which they are linked. Significantly, in all instances, the prime mover behind this development has been the special school headteacher. In all cases they were convinced that the special school pupils would, on the whole, be better catered for in ordinary schools provided that adequate facilities and teaching were made available. The link was seen as a transitional stage designed to ensure that the ordinary school and its teachers were adequately prepared and to establish the requisite support for pupils with special needs in the school.

Selecting schools

In many instances links involve contact between two or more schools which are close to each other, and the question of selecting a partner does not arise for the special school. Choice can be restricted, too, by policies of returning pupils individually to their neighbourhood school or of responding to parents' wishes. There are situations, however, when choices are possible – and, indeed, have to be made. This will happen for instance when special school pupils are moving out individually or where there is more than one possible school in the immediate vicinity. The primary consideration then becomes the characteristics of the available schools.

What criteria did the special schools in our study use when they had a free choice? They fell into three categories: teaching strength, receptiveness and physical layout.

Clearly, the ability to teach pupils is important, and special school staff had to be convinced that the particular learning needs of their pupils were going to be met. Generally, they found it easier to place their academically able pupils since their teaching requirements were closer to those ordinary schools were accustomed to offering. A particular comprehensive school was judged appropriate because it contained a learning support department whose head was enthusiastic about working with pupils with moderate learning difficulties. The department was already running non-examination courses in topics such as skills for living, photography and gardening. Pupils from the special school were able to join these options.

A second criterion was that schools be receptive to pupils with special needs. This is related to the teaching criterion – if the school does not want pupils it is unlikely to take them seriously for teaching purposes – but it is important in its own right as well. Transferring from a small friendly special school to a large secondary school can be traumatic enough without selecting an unwelcoming school at the receiving end. Some special school teachers bemoaned the 'lack of sympathy and unproductive attitude to less able pupils amongst teachers in some mainstream classes'. Some schools on the other hand became known for their positive attitudes toward pupils with special needs and, in consequence, received requests to accommodate them. One headteacher said that 'it was known at County Hall that this school ... would welcome physically handicapped pupils'.

Finally, the physical layout must be considered when pupils with limited mobility are to be accommodated. Suitable schools must allow adequate access – both to the building and within it – to pupils with impaired mobility. They must also allow adequate vehicular access, as demonstrated in the case of one school which, while otherwise appropriate, had to be rejected because the buses transporting physically handicapped pupils from the special school could not be manoeuvred near it.

Selecting pupils

Selecting pupils for participation in a link scheme was generally the responsibility of the special school. Most ordinary school staff were quite happy to leave this task to their special school colleagues. One headteacher of an ordinary school observed that, if the scheme was going to work, there had to be complete trust between the two schools in the link and, in particular, his school had to be prepared to cater for whichever pupils arrived from the special school.

When ordinary schools did exercise choice in which pupils should participate, they did so in fairly ad hoc ways. Note was taken of any information contained in pupil reports or supplied orally and this was related to the educational situation of the ordinary school. One deputy head of a comprehensive school went to meet pupils at the special school in order to assess their suitability for a placement in her school. Generally, any such assessment was informal and relatively unstructured. The main concerns were how pupils would fit into the other school and how their particular needs would be met.

The selection criteria used by special school staff ranged from 'instinct' to the results of sophisticated assessments. Some teachers felt that, on the basis of their contact with pupils in the special school, they knew which of them would manage in other settings and which would not and made their selection accordingly. Others had concerns about pupils' levels of maturity: they should be able to deal with the unfamiliar surroundings of a large school, stand up for themselves among their peers and, interestingly, be able to 'deal with adult inconsistencies'. Pupils' level of attainment in a given subject area was commonly used: if a pupil was to benefit academically without undue levels of support, then he or she had to have a basic competence in the subject area. One school – for pupils with moderate learning difficulties – described a multi-factorial selection procedure based on ability, attainment, social development and maturation, other social factors and length of time at the special school.

Pupil selection depended on the nature of the link scheme and its stage of development. For instance, schemes with a broad remit tended to involve more pupils than schemes intended for a specific purpose. These contrasting approaches are illustrated by the arrangements at Freelands and Standlake respectively. In the first case, the scheme is part of a process of amalgamating schools on the same campus so as to provide a unified service for all pupils. Consequently, pupils are considered for participation in the scheme throughout their school career, and pupils at all stages are involved in classes in the ordinary school. The purpose of the link scheme in the second case is to extend the curricular experience at the secondary stage of the special school pupils in certain respects. Pupils were considered for inclusion only in the context of their annual review. In the event, it was mainly fourth year pupils who participated; they took subject options such as child care and secretarial courses which were available in the comprehensive school.

The stage of development of the scheme was also a factor. Typically, staff were more selective to begin with, partly because the venture was new and they were finding their way and partly because they wanted to 'sell' the scheme by ensuring that the first pupils to participate were successful. A scheme for pupils with severe learning difficulties, for instance, began with the more able and more 'acceptable' pupils. However, as the scheme became established, selection was dropped and all beginners at the special school attended the mainstream nursery. This pattern of moving away from any selection of pupils was found repeatedly elsewhere.

The development of schemes

Link schemes in the case study schools were sufficiently well estab-lished for the participants to have been involved in significant developments for a period of time. During the course of this research some schemes had gained momentum and grown in significance and a number of important issues had been raised in the process. The dynamic nature of some of the links between schools was explicitly referred to by some of those involved. The headteacher of Freelands School said that she found it very difficult to predict exactly what would happen because she envisaged the scheme developing with 'each stage leading perhaps to another unexpected one'. She felt that two years ago she certainly would not have envisaged them doing as much as they were doing and she would not have predicted the very positive attitudes from the ordinary school. The special school has had a joint governing body meeting with the primary school and they were due to have one with the secondary school. They would prepare a paper for the secondary school governors and ask some of the senior special school pupils to stay behind to talk about the link schemes. The headteacher regards this as very much another 'step forward' and said that, although the quantity of integration has gone as far as it can, the quality must be constantly improved. The headteacher of Oakdale School referred to the momentum gained as more and more pupils moved to ordinary schools and said that one significant outcome was that the expectations of some parents for their children had been raised.

Where the link had led to the absorption of the special school into an ordinary school, other issues were raised. In Fyfield House the amalgamation was seen as 'formalizing what has been happening'. There would be a resource centre catering for hearing impaired pupils on the special school site and a management committee would be formed to act in an advisory capacity and to oversee the residential provision. This committee would be represented on the central council meetings for the whole campus.

In this instance the links formed between the schools have been the 'stepping stone' to this amalgamation; the staffing levels have been protected and the posts of headteacher and deputy have been expanded. The former has been employed in an advisory capacity by the authority and the latter is to be head of the resource centre. Concern was expressed by the governors in another school which would eventually be absorbed, that this could result in the pupils having no headteacher or governing body to act on their behalf and to protect their interests. It was suggested that the school could continue to exist in name only so that the governors could continue as a body.

Other issues are raised by the absorption of the senior part of a school. This was the situation at Ashdown School. It was felt to be essential by staff at the receiving school that the pupils should form a department within their school and that they should all integrate for at least some of the time. It was envisaged that the department would serve as a resource for the rest of the school and its newly-appointed head had already collaborated with members of the main school staff about the resources to be purchased. Some equipment and materials held in the department would be made generally available. It was hoped that there would be two-way contact between the department and the host school and all departmental staff would have teaching commitments in the ordinary school.

Factors leading to the development of links

The case study schools illustrated how link schemes could develop as they gained momentum and how staff could facilitate this growth. The headteacher of Oakdale had approached his counterpart in a nearby comprehensive school to ask about placing some of his pupils in special classes because the classes in the primary school were well established and pupils of secondary age would otherwise have to return to the special school site. The positive response resulted in a period of planning and then the transfer of some Oakdale pupils. The deputy headteacher at Freelands School was pleased with the steady progress that had been made. She pointed out that the first pupils to participate had been viewed 'with consternation from some quarters' and the fact that their presence was now fully accepted could be seen as 'a milestone in terms of integration'. The attitude of staff in the comprehensive school was a key factor here. They now felt more confident in dealing with Freelands pupils and had become more positively disposed toward them. It helped that they realized that pupils with physical handicaps were able to cope at their school and that they knew that adequate support was available from Freelands. Another important factor in the development was that Freelands staff had built up experience in operating the scheme. They had seen many pupils through the process and were more aware of possible strategies for success. They were more flexible, for example, about pupils being kept down a year rather than mixing with their chronological peers.

In some instances, the fact that a school has falling rolls may influence the development of links with other establishments. The school may have vacant accommodation that can provide space for new provision, including links. One primary school, that was able to accommodate a group of pupils and their teacher from Larkshill School, regarded this as a way of expanding the school's provision for pupils with learning difficulties. The new arrivals were seen as benefiting the school rather than being a burden on it. Another feature of the development of this arrangement was that the incoming teacher remained on the staff of the special school so that there was no pressure to maintain pupil numbers in the group.

The staff at The Priory School (for pupils with behaviour problems) had given considerable thought to developing their link scheme and cited several lessons they had learnt as it developed. They found that some ordinary school staff were over-confident about their ability to deal with pupils with behaviour problems and sometimes did not sufficiently heed the special school's suggestions. They felt that 'speeding the process is wrong' and that pupils should move into ordinary schools very gradually, with careful monitoring and support. They also expressed concern about outside agencies becoming involved in the process at inappropriate stages and argued that the special school's long-term planning and involvement could be undermined by other professionals coming in at a late stage.

The importance of the staff input to the development of links was frequently referred to. Link teachers needed good organizational and interpersonal skills and should have the ability to work flexibly and establish rapport with colleagues in different work settings. The headteacher of Larkshill School claimed that their link scheme was not 'transportable' because its strength was bound up with the personalities involved and the good rapport that had been established. Where schools were clear about the organizational frameworks and strategies that had been developed to foster the successful movement of pupils, the dependence on particular individuals was less pronounced. The deputy head of one comprehensive school, for example, was very positive about the movement of pupils with special needs to her school and stated that most members of staff had had contact in some way with these pupils. Nobody had ever refused to have a pupil with special needs in a class but she felt that this reflected the groundwork carried out with teachers who were initially apprehensive.

In-service training for teachers of pupils with special needs is discussed in a companion volume (Hegarty and Moses, 1988). Providing training for involved staff was a feature of the development of some link schemes. Freelands School organized regular school-based sessions for teachers in the receiving schools. A comprehensive school hosted a course concerned with hearing impaired pupils. This was spread over several days and was organized on a 'rolling system' so that lectures and demonstrations were repeated on different days to enable teaching staff to attend. The sessions had a strong practical focus and were said to have been well received by the teachers who attended.

Summary

Local authorities embraced link schemes for two sets of reasons; one as a response to falling school rolls and one where links were sought in their own right and established as an integral feature of the authority's special needs provision. Falling rolls are a particular threat to special schools because of their small size and restricted curriculum base – unit costs rise and specific curricular expertise is lost. Some authorities maintained special school staffing levels by giving teachers a range of additional functions such as those involved in running a link scheme or resource centre. A small number of authorities saw the benefits in terms of curriculum protection and enhancement: where a special school lacked specific curricular expertise, this could be supplied by teachers from a linking primary or secondary school.

Many authorities adopted link schemes as valuable in their own right. Sometimes the motivation was to establish a resource centre in special education; the information and training functions implied in this role necessarily led the special schools concerned to develop links with other schools. In other cases the 1981 Act was the stimulus, particularly with respect to providing assessment expertise.

The nature of local authority involvement with link schemes varied from relative passivity to tight control. The different stances taken by the authorities can be grouped under four headings:

1 Reacting to initiatives taken by individual schools
2 Exercising indirect influence, e.g. in new appointments and siting new schools
3 Giving a general policy direction in favour of links but leaving the details to be settled by individual schools
4 Exercising close control and ensuring that link schemes conform to authority policy and mesh with its support services for special needs.

Individual special schools developed link schemes for reasons which paralleled local authorities' reasons for adopting them: on the one hand, falling rolls threatened their very survival, and link schemes offered a possible salvation; on the other hand, many schemes were rooted in a clear concern for children's educational benefit and a desire on the part of the special school staff to make their expertise more widely available.

Choice of ordinary school was frequently limited by geography or policy (e.g. of returning pupils to their neighbourhood school). When free choice was possible, special schools focused on three character- istics of ordinary schools: teaching strength; receptiveness to pupils with special needs; and physical layout. The selection of pupils was generally left in the hands of the special school. Which pupils were selected depended on the nature of the scheme and its stage of development. Staff tended to be cautious at the outset and tried to guarantee success but, as schemes developed, there was less and less selection and pupils who would not previously have been considered were now being included.

5 Administering Link Schemes

Links between special and ordinary schools may entail a great deal of administrative changes in the schools taking part. In some instances these are one-off responses as when transport arrangements for pupils are altered. In other cases there are long-term initiatives that have major organizational implications for the schools concerned as, for example, exchanging and updating information on pupils' progress and ensuring that it is kept up to date. Three main areas of administrative concern are considered in this chapter: preparing pupils to take part in a links programme; implementing pupil links; and organizing the involvement of teachers.

Preparing for pupil links

Link programmes require considerable advance preparation. Once the target pupils have been identified, decisions must be taken on the amount of time they will spend in the ordinary school and individual programmes of work drawn up for them. This can be done on a one-off basis for each pupil, or it can be based on general principles laid down for the link arrangement. The pupils must be prepared for the move, and their parents should be involved. Finally, the receiving school needs to be informed about the pupils concerned and its commitment in respect of them.

Deciding on programmes of work

When agreement has been reached on which pupil(s) should be involved in a link arrangement, the next step is to draw up timetables and programmes of work. In a few cases this is quite straightforward. If a special school class is going to an ordinary school to be taught as an intact group there or if an individual pupil is going out more or less full-time, the main requirement is to find a base in the ordinary school, either an empty classroom or a class that the individual pupil can join. In most cases, however, there is an inter-connected set of decisions to make, focused on the different elements that make up the programme and how it is to be run. These include:

Amount of time. Figures presented in Chapter 2 showed how varied pupils' time allocations in the ordinary school were in the schools surveyed. This was particularly the case for pupils going out individually as opposed to those going out in groups. Most groups spent less than three hours a week in the ordinary school whereas those going out individually were as likely to spend more than 25 hours out each week as they were to spend less than three hours. This variation reflected staff objectives for a given pupil or group, their estimation of how much time in the ordinary school that pupil could cope with and benefit from, and the curriculum choices made.

Whether static or changing. Some links are clearly defined from the outset with a fixed allocation of time and, in some cases, even a time-limit set. When pupils from Standlake School attended some selected lessons to extend their curriculum, the extent of attendance was decided at the outset. Other links, by contrast, work in an exploratory, progressive way: pupils go out for limited periods at first in order to see how they cope with being in an ordinary school and then their timetable is modified in the light of this experience. Pupils from both schools catering for pupils with behaviour problems were introduced into their ordinary schools in this way and, as their confidence increased, their placement was reviewed.

Choice of curriculum area. In some instances pupils were placed in ordinary schools specifically for certain subjects, e.g. secretarial skills or art. When pupils were introduced to an ordinary school in a gradual way, they followed some areas of the mainstream curriculum but not others. Thus, when pupils from Larkshill School formed a satellite class in a primary school, they worked on all their formal curricular activities in this small group but joined their peers for physical education, art and music. More commonly, pupils were attending ordinary schools for set periods of time and took part in the subjects on offer at those times.

Class grouping. Pupils have to be slotted into the academic structure of the ordinary school receiving them. We have seen that this can be done in various ways, ranging from 'satellite' classes from a special school being taught as a group in an ordinary school to individuals joining a normal class in the ordinary school. Two major considerations here were pupils' level of academic achievement and the extent to which appropriate teaching was available in the ordinary school. If a pupil had done very little science, for instance, there would be little point in placing him or her in a large class that was well advanced with a science syllabus and where there was little possibility of individual attention. It was for this reason that so many pupils were placed in slow learner or other bottom sets.

Teachers' freedom of manoeuvre in placing pupils was often constrained in practice by the existing pattern of links or by the academic organization of the receiving school. If there are set ways of grouping pupils from the special school for link purposes, it is likely that individual pupils will be fitted into these arrangements whether they are appropriate or not. As regards the academic organization of the receiving school, it is clear, for example, that mixed ability teaching and rigid streaming allow for very different possibilities. Team teaching is a further case in point. Freelands School provided a member of staff to team teach a group of pupils experiencing difficulties with mathematics in the ordinary school. Two pupils from the special school joined this group.

Support. Many pupils need support, both academic and non-academic, in order to cope with an ordinary school. This is particularly the case when pupils first attend an ordinary school. Hearing impaired pupils, for instance, require long-term support as an essential feature of placement in an ordinary school. If they are joining an ordinary class, academic support may be necessary to fill in gaps in their knowledge where a class has already covered essential background work. Pupils with learning difficulties need long-term support in explaining and reinforcing lesson content. Some pupils require assistance with recording notes from lessons and preparing written assignments, while others need additional supervision during physical education or in practical lessons. Some pupils require help outside the classroom with toileting and mobility.

When pupils' timetables for participation in a link are being drawn up, consideration has to be given to the support they require in the ordinary school and how it is to be provided. As we have seen, a considerable number of teachers and ancillaries from special schools were engaged in providing such support, which they did by working with individual pupils, by team teaching or by teaching combined groups of special school and ordinary school pupils. Adequate staffing to allow flexibility of support is an important factor here. The development of link schemes can be inhibited when such flexibility is not possible. For example, a school which is sending pupils out but is maintaining the same number of teaching groups albeit with smaller numbers is likely to have difficulty in supporting the pupils that do go out. In some such cases pupils received support only if it could be provided from within the ordinary school.

The most intensive support was generally at the beginning of a link. A number of schools had carefully worked out programmes whereby pupils received intensive support at the outset but gradually less and less until it was totally phased out. This was particularly evident in respect of pupils with behaviour problems.

Preparing pupils

Going to a new school is a daunting experience for many pupils. It can be particularly so for pupils who have difficulty in school anyway and the transition is from a familiar special school to a large and alien ordinary school. Some schools sought to ease the transition by having pupils' prospective teachers come to meet them in the special school. Another step was to familiarize pupils in advance with the physical layout of the school, canteen arrangements and so on. These initiatives were valuable in allaying anxieties and helping pupils to settle down. One school had a programme of counselling pupils so that their fears and worries could be aired and they could be helped to come to terms with them.

Involving parents

Most parents were reported to be pleased, although often rather apprehensive, about the opportunity provided for their child by a link scheme. Parents interviewed for this research were mostly enthusiastic and they felt that the schools in question had involved them in the early stages of discussion and had kept them informed of developments in their child's placement. The schools were characterized by high levels of contact with parents and there were well-established channels of communication. Movement to an ordinary school was commonly seen as a sign of progress having been made by the child concerned and parents were positive about the move. The parents of one child with behaviour problems were dissatisfied in that they did not feel that he would benefit from moving into an ordinary school for his final year and they considered that the decision had been made for them.

Developing productive relationships with, and being accessible to, parents when pupils are involved in link schemes is one aspect of managing the movement of pupils. One parent who experienced considerable difficulty in meeting new people and was reluctant to leave her house any more than was necessary had been visited by teachers from both of the schools involved in her son's link programme. It was clear that the schools had made an effort to establish a relationship with her and she certainly felt that she had been consulted and informed about her son's transfer. The parents of another boy from the same special school felt that they could contact the special school about any aspect of their son's part-time placement in an ordinary school. They had, for instance, telephoned the support teacher at the special school to discuss the difficulties with note-taking that their son was having and found him to be very approachable. They were confident that he would try to resolve any problems on his visits to the ordinary school and were appreciative of his efforts.

The significance of effective communication with parents was highlighted by the experience of one parent in particular. Her son had been referred to a unit from his primary school and her contact with the unit teacher had initially been very constructive. The latter had been optimistic about her son's potential and promised to keep her informed of his progress. The boy did not appear to benefit from the unit and was offered a special school place. His mother saw this as putting him on a 'downward spiral' and was very concerned that the initial positive approach from the unit teacher had not been consolidated. She was not happy about the transfer to special school and felt that she had been excluded from any decision-making. She had had contact with the unit teacher on only one occasion. After this experience, the very welcoming and helpful approach that she perceived from the special school staff was particularly appreciated when her son became involved in the link scheme.

Informing the ordinary school

Apart from those situations where ordinary school staff have been closely involved in selecting pupils to participate in link arrangements, the special school must convey appropriate information to the ordinary school about the pupils concerned. The kind and amount of detail necessary vary with the nature of the link and its stage of development. Typically, when a link arrangement is starting up and both sets of staff are relatively unfamiliar with each other's routines and procedures, there is greater need of information sharing than later on.

The information to be transmitted is of two types, dealing respectively with the pupils and with the link arrangement. The first requirement obviously is that the ordinary school be told which pupils are coming, for which subjects and for how long. This can be usefully supplemented with information on each pupil's patterns of difficulty in learning or adjustment. In the case of pupils with physical or sensory impairments, the ordinary school needs to be given any information that has a bearing on the pupils' education. Special schools often have information on family background and pupils' personal situation which may need to be communicated as well.

The second type of information has to do with the link arrangement in a broader way. Staff may be uncertain about what is intended for the arrangement and how precisely it should operate in their school. A clear statement setting out the parameters of the arrangement and detailing its working procedures helps to resolve this uncertainty. It is particularly helpful if clear lines of responsibility are laid down for pupils who are dividing their time between the two schools, and ordinary school staff know who to contact in the special school, should the need arise. Guidelines on teaching pupils from the special school are sometimes issued. These can be helpful if staff in the ordinary school are not familiar with the patterns of behaviour or learning difficulty exhibited by the pupils they are receiving.

How did special schools actually communicate this information and what constraints did they experience in doing so? Many schools transmitted basic information by written means. They circulated lists giving brief particulars on each pupil and, perhaps, some details on teaching them. This did raise questions of confidentiality and respect for pupils' privacy when such written information was circulated widely. This is not a new problem for schools, especially large secondary schools, but the issues raised are particularly pointed in the case of pupils with special needs.

The approach of Freelands School (for physically handicapped pupils) was to couch information in general terms, pointing out, for instance, that double incontinence could be a feature of life for those with spina bifida but without naming pupils who were incontinent. This particular school went to considerable lengths to provide information about the nature of pupils' handicapping conditions and how the link arrangement was intended to operate. A booklet was produced about integrating pupils into mainstream classes with their particular pupils centrally in mind. It was scheduled to be updated regularly as the link developed. The booklet contains brief details on cerebral palsy, spina bifida, brittle bone disease, muscular dystrophy and brain tumours, and refers to some educational implications of these conditions. There are some general statements about physical handicap, e.g.

Physically handicapped children are not necessary sickly, but they may be hospitalised from time to time for surgery and all attend hospital regularly for routine check-ups.

The booklet also contains practical information about the link arrangements, e.g.

All Freelands pupils are brought to school and taken home by transport provided by the Local Authority. The mini buses leave Freelands at 3.30pm sharp and it is not usually possible for Freelands pupils to stay after school.

Freelands pupils return to the school when they are not timetabled in the ordinary school. They all have one period in our swimming pool and in any of the remaining periods they have therapy as appropriate and private study. If a pupil is behind with work this can be an opportunity for catching up.

In general, the booklet seeks to convey a positive picture of the link, stressing the cooperation between the two sets of staff that is entailed. It acknowledges the essential contribution of the ordinary school staff and affirms the intention of the special school to provide advice and support. In confirmation of the latter, staff's telephone extension numbers at the special school are listed.

A few special schools provided written guidelines on teaching pupils with special needs, though they seldom amounted to more than teaching 'tips'. These might be related to the particular pupils who were the subject of the link or they might be couched in a more general way. Some special school teachers felt that, as their pupils were academically able, it would be inappropriate to instruct their colleagues on how to teach them.

A good deal of information was transmitted by more direct means as well, and some schools did not, in fact, commit anything to paper. One approach used when pupils were being placed individually was to give a briefing on each of them to the relevant staff in the ordinary school. Apart from setting up contact with colleagues from the special school, this gave ordinary school teachers the opportunity to ask questions and relate the information being given to their particular teaching circumstances. When joint case conferences were a feature of the link arrangements they were an important means of sharing information. In some cases there were lectures about the link arrangement which served the purpose of describing it as well as generating enthusiasm for it. Some special schools appointed liaison teachers for the link, part of whose function was to give any necessary information to colleagues at the ordinary school about the pupils they were receiving.

Views were not unanimous on the amount of information that should be transmitted. Some ordinary school teachers were willing to accept special school pupils into their class but did not want background information on them nor did they wish to discuss them with special school staff. By contrast, staff in one comprehensive school were very concerned over the dearth of information available to them. A key factor here seemed to be the degree of responsibility that staff felt for pupils. When pupils were accompanied by ancillary staff or received extensive support from the special school in other ways, ordinary school teachers were less likely to seek out information than if they felt they had sole responsibility for pupils.

Implementing pupil links

Once pupils have been selected to take part in a link, programmes of work devised for them and everybody's involvement secured, the next step is to implement the link. The pupils must be introduced to the ordinary school. Practical matters relating to access and accommodation need to be arranged. Timetabling adjustments may be necessary at both schools. Necessary resources must be made available. Procedures for gathering and sharing information must be established and, if appropriate, used to modify pupils' programmes of work.

Introducing pupils to the ordinary school

How pupils were introduced to the ordinary school depended on how many there were and the type of programme envisaged for them. When it was just one or a very few pupils, they might well be accompanied by a teacher or ancillary from the special school who would introduce them to the class or classes they were going to join and then withdraw. Similarly, if pupils were going to an ordinary school for a limited period only, there was often felt to be less need of extensive introductions.

When schools engaged in substantial programmes of pupil links, the process of introducing pupils and phasing them into the ordinary school was generally given more time and attention. Typically, such programmes started on a gradual basis. To begin with, pupils attended the ordinary school for relatively short periods, possibly supported by a teacher or classroom assistant from the special school. If all went well, the time spent in the ordinary school increased and the amount of support decreased. In some cases there was a formal trial period, lasting a month or so, at the end of which all the staff involved reviewed progress and made a decision as to how to proceed on a long-term basis. This had the advantage that a link could be abandoned without fuss and the pupil returned full time to the special school if that was the course of action indicated. It was judged important for staff to approach these initial stages in a tentative exploratory way, gauging the amount of support pupils needed and pulling back when appropriate so that pupils could make their own way.

One school instituted a form of peer support. Each pupil from the special school was paired with a fellow pupil from the ordinary school who was made responsible for bringing him or her to the ordinary school initially and generally for smoothing initial difficulties.

Access and accommodation

Many special school pupils travel to and from school on special transport. This often runs to a fairly inflexible schedule and changes may have to be made if the two schools have different times for starting and finishing the school day. An alternative problem is when the special transport is erratic: pupils' participation in a link programme can be adversely affected if they are frequently late for school, whereas the special school can generally cope more flexibly with irregular arrivals. In the link arrangements studied, pupils from the special school often left the ordinary school early in order to be on time for their transport home. In one case, pupils consistently arrived late at the ordinary school and also left half an hour early.

Transport between the participating schools is another consideration. Unless the two schools are literally adjacent, with a linking corridor, flexibility becomes a major issue. Short distances can obviously be negotiated without too much difficulty. As the distance separating the schools grows, so do the logistical difficulties of moving pupils about. Beyond a certain limit the difficulties become prohibitive; pupils cannot move readily from school to school in the course of the school day and only full-time placements may be possible. All these problems become more acute in the case of pupils with impaired mobility, whether this be due to physical or sensory impairment. In the case of the former, any special transport required to bring pupils to school may need to be available throughout the school day as well.

Where pupils are moving out for parts of the school day, procedures for recording absences may need to be instituted. If the number of pupils concerned is small, the requisite information can be transmitted on a direct teacher-to-teacher basis. As the number of pupils grows, however, or if they go to many different classes, a formal procedure for passing on information is necessary.

An incident was recalled in one large comprehensive school where a class teacher had left his group of 30 pupils to search for one physically handicapped pupil who, his peers said, was probably on his way in his wheelchair. The pupil was suffering from a progressive muscular disorder and the teacher was very concerned about his whereabouts. On reaching the special school he was informed that the boy was in fact absent on that day. As a result of this and other related incidents, a formal procedure was instituted. The special school now telephones the reception area in the comprehensive school at 9.00 each morning to report any pupils who will not be attending. Somebody from reception is responsible for passing on these names to the class teachers concerned. On a related point, the special school staff now send across timetables of individual special school pupils who are attending classes so that their overall movement can be monitored.

Staff at another special school have recently revised the system for recording absences and have made it the responsibility of one particular welfare assistant. When the school buses arrive in the morning, note is made of any absences, using pre-printed lists. The welfare assistant collects these lists and marks any senior pupils' absences on a list printed in triplicate. One copy goes to the deputy head of the special school and two are taken to the comprehensive school where one is pinned on the staff notice board and another goes to the deputy head there. Pupils are given explicit responsibility for informing staff about any lateness for classes on their part.

Access to the ordinary school was sometimes an issue where pupils with physical handicaps were concerned. Some schools built ramps and modified toilets. There were instances where staff said that a liberal interpretation of fire regulations was necessary. If the regulations were followed strictly to the letter, pupil mobility would be severely restricted – unless major, and prohibitively expensive, building works were carried out.

Room allocation could be a further source of difficulty where pupils with physical handicaps were concerned. Thus, if laboratories or other rooms with specialist equipment are not on the ground floor and some pupils are confined to the ground floor, problems are inevitable. There is a danger that the class which special school pupils are joining will be sold short on practical work since they do not have automatic access to every part of the school. Teachers can move equipment and books around but this is not popular and, in any case, is not possible with much science and craft equipment. Teachers interviewed in one school receiving pupils from a school for pupils with physical handicaps were quite vociferous about the limitations imposed on them in this way. One added that 'it doesn't do much for the status of A-level geography if students are studying for it in a broom cupboard!'

Timetable adjustments

Two schools in our study that were endeavouring to run a link programme for pupils had school days of four periods and seven periods respectively! If pupils are to split their time between two schools, it is far easier to do so if the schools start and finish at the same time, have common lunch and break times and, above all, divide the day into the same units of time. This would suggest that schools should harmonize their timetables if they are planning a substantial programme of pupil links. One case study headteacher prepared her timetable during the summer when she had received copies of the timetables from the ordinary schools in the link scheme.

Harmonizing timetables can be difficult, however. It was usually seen as something for the special school – rather than the ordinary school – to do, since the former was the one taking the initiative and was in any case much smaller. When a special school was linking up with several different ordinary schools, harmonization might simply be impossible because of the difference between the schools. In the more usual situation, where a special school had a substantial link with only one ordinary school, there could still be problems.

Transport difficulties have been mentioned already, and these can certainly be exacerbated if the special school starts later or finishes earlier than the ordinary school. If break times do not coincide, pupils may lose the opportunity for peer contact which can be a valuable part of the link. The principal requirement, however, is to create a framework that will allow pupils to have a coherent experience of the curriculum.

The staff of one case study school were keen to stress that having pupils involved in placements in other schools did not diminish their workload but, in fact, meant that they had to 'redirect energies'. The deputy head of another school said that it is a 'nightmare' trying to organize their pupils' placements effectively and felt that 'a lot of teachers would not put up with all the extra work'. The headteacher of this school stated that he often started work at 8am simply to cope with the administration. Staff in the receiving schools need advance notice of which pupils are coming to them if they are to to plan placements, and organize classes effectively. One deputy head, for example, said that she was careful to keep numbers relatively low in a group if she knew in advance that some children in wheelchairs would be attending. Another felt that special school staff did not always understand the complexity of certain subject options or realize the background knowledge needed to take some courses. She referred to one boy who could not be slotted into science in the fourth year because his three years at the special school had not geared him for the Nuffield syllabus followed in the comprehensive school. One headteacher of a special school was well aware of the organizational implications for schools taking her pupils and she was committed to a flexible approach from her school to fit in with arrangements at the larger ordinary school.

The timetable and the academic structure which it embodies reflect a school's curriculum. When two schools have very different philosophies and curricular orientations it is to be expected that their timetables will be correspondingly different. It may well happen that only by a major re-think of its own curriculum and academic purposes can the special school bring its timetable into line with that of the ordinary school. At a more mundane level, the special school may be hampered in making the necessary changes because of its staffing limitations and the internal logistics of providing a coherent programme of work for all its pupils. Pupils going out for a particular set of subjects must do so at times dictated by the ordinary school and the balance of their programme of work, provided in the special school, must be fitted into the time remaining. This can result in considerable pressure on the special school, particularly if some of the staff are engaged in supporting the pupils going to the ordinary school.

Resources

Schools are resourced, through staffing establishments and pupil capitation, on the basis of the number of pupils on roll and the educational needs they present. When pupils are dividing their time between schools, the resourcing arrangements have to be modified accordingly. This is particularly important at a time when there is pressure on resources. If pupils make more than usual demands without, as it were, paying their way, negative attitudes can be expected. The resource implications of a link arrangement must, therefore, be explicitly recognized so that the ordinary school receives appropriate compensation for the extra demands made on it.

The most obvious resource for any link is staff. There were case study schools where extra staff were available to the associated ordinary schools. One school, receiving a considerable number of physically handicapped pupils, had a small extra allocation of teaching staff to allow for this. Another had recently appointed a classroom assistant allocated by the local authority as a response to the demands made on them by the link scheme. The link involving Elm Grange was designed to provide support by staff for ordinary school teachers. One adviser hoped to negotiate a situation whereby pupils involved in substantial links were counted twice for capitation purposes – once for the special school and once for the ordinary school.

The question of compensating ordinary schools for the pupils they take from other schools loomed large in many link arrangements. The deputy head of one school pointed to the concern among staff that they were not being given appropriate resources. She referred to one full-time sixth former who was still counted on the special school roll and said that she could reasonably be included on the ordinary school roll. A number of special schools took ad hoc steps to show goodwill to the receiving schools. One placed a welfare assistant at the disposal of a primary school for half a day a week, which she spent working in classes not containing pupils from the special school. Another special school bought equipment for the use of all pupils in the ordinary school with which it was linked. This included display cabinets and tilting tables that could be used by all pupils.

It should be realized that link arrangements can add to the resource requirements and, therefore, the costs of educating pupils with special needs. Direct resource increments include additional staff time in liaising between schools, monitoring pupils' programmes across two schools and providing in-service training, building modifications, and duplication of material resources. Standlake School (for pupils with physical handicaps) acquired six motorized scooters to enable pupils to travel the short but exposed path between the two schools. A major source of additional indirect expenditure is when special school teachers support pupils in the ordinary school but the same number of teaching groups is still required in the special school. As a general rule, the effective reduction in pupil numbers at a special school is seldom translated into a corresponding saving – even though the process itself entails considerable extra expenditure.

Very practical issues are raised when pupils who need particular resources are spending time in ordinary schools in that the resources may not be easily transferable as the pupils progress through the school. In the case study scheme for pupils from Oakdale School the route is relatively clear for them to transfer through ordinary classes. The younger children have a classroom with plenty of space for equipment and changing facilities and the junior pupils are housed in an ordinary classroom. Children who need to be changed and to use large-scale equipment cannot be accommodated with their age peers as the space is presently organized. Clearly there were administrative decisions for schools to make in relation to purchasing specific equipment or aids to facilitate link schemes. Buildings may need modifying and certain pieces of equipment may be required.

Even when staff are directly involved in negotiating support for pupils, many have very little knowledge of the relevant administrative structures or of the finances that are potentially available to them. One headteacher, for example, said that he knew very little about how link arrangements were financed and he anticipated long-term negotiations with officers in the authority in relation to the resources he required. The adviser for special needs in the same authority acknowledged that he had very little idea where finances came from and was sometimes uncertain 'whether to push for money to get things done properly' or to 'scrimp and be acceptable to the authority'.

Monitoring progress

Monitoring progress is particularly important in the education of pupils with special needs since their programmes of work tend to be complex and to require regular revision in the light of experience. This is often one of the weaknesses of special education programmes even when they are contained within a single school. When pupils divide their time between two schools and two sets of teachers, it becomes more problematic still but also more important – there is less likely to be informal contact between the teachers, and it may well turn out that no one person has the overall picture of a pupil's progress.

How did schools in our study achieve this cross-school monitoring, and what problems were encountered in doing so? It should be noted that this was not an issue at either end of the spectrum of link arrangements. When special school pupils were integrated for short periods only and remained the responsibility of special school staff during that time, there were no new problems of monitoring and when pupils were full time, or nearly full time in the ordinary school, they became, effectively, the ordinary school's responsibility and fell within its arrangements for monitoring progress. It was between these extremes, when special school pupils spent a considerable proportion but not all of the week in an ordinary school, that special steps had to be taken to monitor progress.

There were three aspects to this: written records of the work pupils covered in the different settings, their achievements and any problems; sharing this written information; discussing pupils, either formally and on the basis of written reports, or informally. Where the links could lead to the transfer of a pupil to an ordinary school, staff from the receiving school were invited to meetings to discuss progress. Where staff from the special school maintained the responsibility for the pupils, the process of recording and sharing information was not so developed. At one extreme, the close contact between Freelands School and the neighbouring comprehensive school was said to facilitate easy communication between staff and, in addition to standard reviews of progress there was regular contact when pupils were causing concern. At the other extreme, staff in two schools joined in a link scheme were very concerned about the lack of contact and there was considerable unease among the teachers involved.

Where pupils are spending time in two schools, responsibility for aspects of their care and education may need to be allocated explicitly. One school for physically handicapped pupils, for example, had primary age children attending an ordinary school for part of their timetable, and they had decided to limit these visits to the afternoons because it had proved to be too difficult to share responsibility for the academic progress of the children. The various activities covered in the afternoon sessions could be more easily accommodated in the pupils' timetables. For older pupils spending time in the comprehensive school, it was explicitly stated that staff at the special school were responsible for any specialized requirements their pupils might have. The deputy headteacher at the comprehensive school said that she felt this was appropriate and that having such a clear division of responsibility simplified arrangements. Special school staff were responsible for any help with toileting that pupils might require and for ensuring that support was available in classrooms when appropriate. Welfare assistants came from the special school to provide physical assistance in lessons when required.

In the Oakdale link, where classes of children with severe learning difficulties worked with their teachers in ordinary schools, the total responsibility for them rested with the Oakdale teachers. Pupils might move from their special classes to ordinary ones for part of their time, but responsibility for their work, care and integration within the school was very firmly the responsibility of their class teacher. While this may have simplified dealings in the short-term, the headteacher of the special school was concerned that this divide perpetuated a situation where the special classes were 'visitors', albeit very welcome and accepted ones. The headteacher said that if the special school were to close and pupils were officially transferred to the roll of an ordinary school, then they would become administratively part of the school and functional integration might be facilitated.

Monitoring progress and writing reports may be viewed very differently by staff in different schools. Both 'sides' in the Standlake scheme were concerned about the system used to communicate about individual pupils. The deputy headteacher of the comprehensive school had attended some review meetings as a representative of the school. She said that very little time had been allocated to the discussion of each pupil, and their parents had been in the room for only a matter of minutes. She felt that the reports were insufficiently detailed and the level of discussion was poor. Conversely, the deputy headteacher of the special school reported that the subject graded reports of the ordinary school seemed very limited to her staff who were used to dealing in detailed reports of the 'whole child'.

In another scheme, where visiting special school teachers withdrew pupils from their classes to work with them, the teachers had very clear procedures for record-keeping and they centralized information in their log books. Each visit was carefully documented in terms of which pupils attended, what work was undertaken with them and which worksheets were distributed. There were records of each pupil's test results, suggestions for a programme of work and comments about their particular areas of difficulty. All this information was photocopied and passed on to class teachers for their use.

When there is contact between two or more schools, channels to facilitate on-going exchanges of information are important in relation to both individual pupils and practical arrangements. Information about pupils' progress and plans needs to be communicated to all members of staff involved with them. As links develop between different establishments, difficulties may arise concerning such matters as accommodation and timetabling. In one comprehensive school taking pupils from a case study school, for example, considerable concern was expressed about the lack of information available from the special school. Timetables of individual special school pupils held at the comprehensive school were out of date, and there were two instances recorded when pupils had moved on to further education without the ordinary school staff being officially informed. The deputy head said that she was in a rather awkward position in that class teachers did not pass on information about individual pupils to her because they assumed that she was communicating regularly with the special school staff and she did not wish to let them know how little she was told. She was concerned that teachers felt that their work with special school pupils was not appreciated by the special school staff and did not wish to reinforce this situation by giving voice to her own dissatisfactions.

Another related point concerns the availability of previously confidential information once pupils are attending two schools. The teacher in one primary school, who was responsible for contacts with a special school, was very pleased that they had recently been allowed access to the files of pupils coming to them. She said that if teachers in two schools are dealing with the same children they need 'the background information'. She said that 'they need to know the danger signs to look for and to know possible reasons why a child is, for example, falling asleep'. The headteacher of one special school felt that since most of his pupils only attended the ordinary school part-time their files were the responsibility of the special school. He stated that 'all information is available' to the comprehensive school and that he would prefer it to be transmitted in 'face to face exchanges between teachers'. He emphasized that it is the special school's responsibility to be selective about information, as 'a lot of it can work against a child'.

Staff involvement

Link schemes depend on the input made by teachers and ancillaries. If a scheme has any size or complexity, this input can have considerable administrative implications. Two areas are considered here: making decisions on staffing levels and organizing teacher involvement.

Staffing for link schemes

Organizational aspects of staff involvement in more than one school include both the setting of staffing levels to accommodate the work and the allocation of responsibility for certain tasks within the schools. On the first point, staff in several case study schools stressed that having some of their pupils taught in other schools did not necessarily mean that they were freed from teaching commitments. Those pupils who remained in the special school still required the same breadth of teaching even though classes were smaller when some pupils were in other schools. It was also pointed out that sufficient staff were required to enable some pupils to be accompanied to ordinary classes. When welfare assistants were accompanying pupils elsewhere, they were obviously not available for deployment within the special school. It is of interest that, when pupils attended ordinary schools for integrated sessions, they were often accompanied by a teacher. Work in the case study schools would suggest that pupils could attend these sessions with a welfare assistant, thereby enabling the teacher to continue work with the pupils remaining.

In some arrangements, staff were involved in links as part of their standard timetable and, in others, staff had time available to them because of falling rolls within the school. In other instances, extra staffing had been made available. In one authority, for example, two teachers had been allocated to the two special schools that were providing teachers to support pupils in ordinary schools. The staffing costs and extra finance for the materials they prepared for these sessions had been drawn from the authority's Research and Development budget. One case study school had been allocated an extra welfare assistant to allow for the increased use of micro-technology and its transportation between schools with individual pupils.

Allocating responsibility for the work involved in links between schools was another aspect of their daily administration. In one authority schools were required to nominate a 'key person' to be responsible for provision for pupils with special needs. If the job description they provided involved an extension of an individual's workload, they were allocated extra staffing points to enable them to make this provision. In the case study schools there were clear lines of responsibility for work with other schools. In some instances this work formed a substantial proportion of teachers' timetables and, in others, teachers were given a supervisory responsibility which might or might not include direct work with the pupils involved. It was usual for a senior member of staff to be responsible for any liaison concerning the link between their school and ordinary schools.

Ordinary schools, too, generally had a designated teacher responsible for the link programme. These teachers were the first point of contact for special school staff on all matters relating to the link. Special school staff would approach the designated teacher when they felt a pupil was nearly ready for an ordinary school placement. The designated teacher would suggest which class teacher to approach and generally act as a facilitator and channel of communication when link programmes were running.

The importance of designating a teacher who can be timetabled for the necessary commitment is highlighted by the experience of a comprehensive school where the deputy head acted as the designated teacher. The school was allocated a welfare assistant to support pupils with physical handicaps who were coming to the school as part of a link arrangement. The welfare assistant needed close supervision on a day-to-day basis, and this intruded on the deputy head's other work. For a while, staff found that their access to the deputy head was severely restricted because of the amount of her time taken up by the welfare assistant and the link programme.

Organizing teacher involvement

It was clear from work undertaken in the schools that organizing teachers' days could be problematic when they were working in more than one school. Planning visits to schools to secure the optimum use of time and resources requires careful organization. In one special school studied, where many pupils were in classes in two ordinary schools, the headteacher spent a great deal of time travelling between schools. Some of the classrooms used contained telephones so that direct contact could be easily made.

Planning a day of travelling around schools may be difficult given the complex and unpredictable nature of life in many schools. Teachers who spent much of their timetable supporting individual pupils in ordinary schools found that their plans were often thwarted. Disruptions to their contact with teachers were caused when teachers were absent or were engaged in other school business at the time of their visit. The emphasis for the support work is on the pupil but staff need some contact with teachers as well and it may be inappropriate to have this during lesson time. During one particular support visit the teacher chatted to the special school pupil during the lunch-break and then followed him into a maths lesson. The pupil, who participated fully in the discussion of mathematical concepts, was very able and was receiving emotional rather than curriculum support from this visit. Then there was some discussion between the teachers about arrangements for the pupil to go on a school trip.

Finding the appropriate time to discuss day-to-day arrangements is sometimes difficult and the need for forward planning was frequently demonstrated in the course of this research. In schemes where teachers visit ordinary schools there may be productive liaison and agreement between the headteachers involved but, unless this is matched by a sharing of information among staff, there can be considerable confusion in practice. Special school staff have sometimes arrived unexpectedly in classes; at other times subject teachers have not been available to talk to them because they have not been informed when the visits were arranged. Concern was also expressed that the purpose of visits by support staff was sometimes not clear.

Coordinating timetables when staff are working in more than one school can be problematic. Arranging pupils' and teachers' timetables so that teachers' time is used most effectively may require considerable thought. In one case study school, the teacher going into ordinary classes to withdraw pupils had only two or three pupils to teach for a substantial part of her time in that school. The external groups run by staff from one case study school sometimes required the teachers to travel several miles to the ordinary school, only to find a very depleted group of pupils waiting for them. As 'outsiders' they had less influence over pupils' attendance than if they were working in the main school. Links involving secondary schools may be particularly problematic because of their mode of organization. The designated liaison teacher at the ordinary school may not teach the individual pupils under discussion. Staff working with pupils with behavioural problems who attended two schools felt that it would be impossible to operate specific programmes of behaviour modification in secondary schools, given the organizational constraints, unless they could liaise with helpful, individual members of staff.

One teacher, in a school for pupils with behaviour problems, had one day a week free to support pupils going out to ordinary primary schools by liaising with their teachers. She made appointments to follow individual pupils and she went to schools in response to requests for advice. She also engaged in what she referred to as 'trouble-shooting' and lamented the fact that schools were very slow to call her in so that difficulties had built up to an explosive pitch when she did get there. One senior teacher at the school expressed concern about the use of the support time and felt that there was a superfluous managerial layer in the school's structure so that class teachers did not feel that they had responsibility for their pupils. She also felt that there was inadequate supervision of the use of support time.

Summary

Link schemes affect the structure and running of the participant schools and may require a good deal of administrative action. This has been considered here in terms of the steps taken to prepare pupils for moving out from the special school to an ordinary school, the actual implementation of link programmes and staffing arrangements.

Preparing for pupil links entailed an interconnected set of decisions focused on pupils' programmes of work. These had to take account of: the amount of time pupils would spend out in the ordinary school and whether this would change in time; choice of curriculum areas; the teaching arrangements and class grouping deemed appropriate and any requirement for special support. Schools acknowledged that a link programme could be a daunting experience for pupils and adopted various expedients to ease the transition for them. Involving parents and developing productive relationships with them were given high priority by some schools in their preparatory work.

Finally, information about the pupils and the link arrangement must be given by the special school to the ordinary school. The latter must know which pupils are coming, for what subjects and for how long. This was often supplemented with information on pupils' patterns of difficulty in learning or adjustment. The amount of information actually given and the mode of delivery varied greatly. Some schools circulated extensive written information – details on each pupil, information on relevant handicapping conditions and guidelines on teaching pupils with special needs. Others preferred to pass on information in direct briefing of colleagues and committed very little to paper.

Implementing a programme of pupil links entailed a range of practical steps. These varied according to the nature and extent of the programme, but experience showed that careful attention to them contributed to the success of programmes. Pupils tended to be introduced to their ordinary school placement gradually, with initial intensive support being phased out over a period of time. Access and transport, accommodation and resources, all required attention and, in some cases, called for considerable administrative action. Differences in the start and finish and duration of the school day led to major difficulties; clear advantages were gained from harmonizing the timetables of linking schools and, when this was not possible, pupils faced another level of difficulty.

Monitoring pupils' progress in a link scheme is complicated by the fact that they attend two schools and will be taught by two sets of teachers. Schools found it important to lay down clear lines of responsibility for pupils' education, establish procedures for collecting information on the work pupils did in the different settings and how well they got on and to ensure that this information was shared with relevant colleagues.

Link schemes raise numerous administrative matters bearing on staff. Two in particular stood out: making decisions on staffing levels and organizing teacher involvement. Many special schools found that an extensive link programme entailed an element of double staffing, in that pupils required support in the ordinary school and, for those pupils not participating in the link, the same range of curriculum had to be offered in the special school. When staff did work in a school or schools other than their own, fragmentation of effort could sometimes be a problem and careful planning was necessary to make sure that best use was made of their time. Lines of responsibility were sometimes confused when staff spent most of their time away from their base school; here, too, problems could be avoided by explicitly setting down duties and reporting procedures.

6 The Implications of Link Schemes for Teachers

Some of the administrative and organizational aspects of the involvement of teachers in link schemes have been discussed in the previous chapter. The implications for staff whose working patterns are altered because of arrangements made between their school and one or more other schools are described here. These implications vary according to the nature of the link, the proportion of the teachers' time allocated to it and whether they are from special or ordinary schools. The findings presented in Chapter 2 showed the extent to which teachers were in contact with other schools and the work that they undertook; this chapter describes how these links worked in practice, as far as teachers from both special schools and ordinary schools were concerned.

The first section of this chapter discusses the work undertaken by special school teachers who regularly spent part of their working week in ordinary schools. Much of their time was spent in teaching or providing emotional support for pupils taking part in link schemes. Some teachers sought to pass on teaching techniques and their experience of working with pupils with special needs to their colleagues. In any case, link schemes involve a wide range of contacts with colleagues, with attendant satisfactions and frustrations for those involved. The second section of the chapter describes arrangements where teachers from special schools experienced a change of working environment in that they were based in ordinary schools although still employed by the special school. The final section is concerned with the situation of teachers in ordinary schools who received pupils from special schools into their classes.

Special school teachers working in ordinary schools

Figures presented in Chapter 2 showed that about a third of the special schools responding to the questionnaire had teachers spending time in ordinary schools on a regular weekly basis. Three-quarters of these teachers were spending less than five hours a week engaged in this work. As against that, the remaining quarter were working outside their own school for one or more days a week and, in a few cases, were spending the entire week working in other schools. When teachers went out, two-thirds of their time was spent teaching pupils. The most frequently occurring activity was teaching groups containing pupils from both the ordinary school and the special school. Nearly a third of teachers' time was spent advising colleagues in the ordinary school on the teaching and management of pupils with special educational needs. Details of these activities drawn from the case study schools and some of the personal and professional implications for the staff involved are presented here.

Teaching pupils

In some of the case study schemes, the working week of teachers had been substantially altered and their duties were very different from those of a classroom teacher. Some taught pupils from the special school attending ordinary classes. Others worked with groups comprising pupils from the receiving school or with groups containing pupils from both schools.

The deputy headteacher of Freelands School taught French to combined groups each week; one of her colleagues taught on a communications course for senior pupils in the comprehensive school. Teachers from both Larkshill School and Elm Grange School spent much of their working week in ordinary schools. They taught a range of subjects including life skills, oral communication and mathematics. Much of their work was undertaken with groups withdrawn from their classes, although they did assist in the classroom with some mixed ability groups.

It was intended that teachers from Ashdown School would be teaching both integrated and segregated groups as their work in the ordinary school expanded following amalgamation. Likewise, opportunities for teaching both the special school pupils they were primarily responsible for and pupils from the ordinary school would increase as the arrangements made for the Larkshill teachers and those from Fyfield House became more established. These three arrangements are described in the second section of this chapter.

Teachers in ordinary schools, notably those taking subjects with a practical component, welcomed this help. In some cases, they had several pupils experiencing difficulty in their classes, not just those who had transferred from the special school. The presence of the support teachers served to increase the amount of pupil withdrawal. There was often no evidence of teachers in the ordinary schools becoming better equipped to work with less able pupils. Pupils were withdrawn for much of their academic work in some schools because it was felt that adequate provision was not currently made for them. Focusing on the needs of classroom teachers in their work with less able pupils might be a more productive strategy, and some schools did, of course, adopt and develop this approach.

One feature of the teaching provided by special school teachers is that it may serve to identify pupils who are later transferred to a special school. This can happen if a pupil is not responding to the provision available in the ordinary school and staff judge that a special school placement would be more beneficial. Ironically, it can also happen if pupils are actually making progress. There were instances of pupils making so much progress with the 'extra' work provided by special school staff that staff felt they would benefit from the concentrated exposure to such work that would be possible in a special school. One headteacher summed up a common response when he said that he did not feel that support work would result in fewer children going to special school – there would 'always be children who need a special environment'. The links 'should help teachers to be better at picking out children who would benefit and will help them to cope with the great many children who have difficulties'.

Supporting pupils

Teachers from special schools provided emotional support for their pupils who were spending time in ordinary schools. They helped the pupils to make a smooth transition to the new setting by providing them with practical help and by being present during the initial stages of the transfer. The emphasis was primarily on providing a sense of continuity for the special school pupil and not on supporting or assisting the ordinary school teacher.

The deputy head of The Priory School underlined the importance of personal support for pupils – those who had gone to ordinary schools without support had 'floundered' and seemed lost, whereas those with support teachers had benefited from 'the continual support of trusting adults they know'. In the latter case, problems were 'ironed out on the spot' and pupils settled in more easily. This focus on support for pupils rather than teachers was exemplified in an art lesson observed in a primary school which received pupils from The Priory School.

> John was in an art lesson in the primary school which he attended for one day a week. The support teacher stood at the back of the class chatting at intervals to John and two or three other boys. There was little contact with the class teacher other than a very short exchange about progress in the school. The support teacher was not involved in the lesson at all and the work did not require consolidation or further explanation at the special school. The teacher in this class was experienced and skilled in classroom organization, managing to keep a group of more than 20 juniors working independently on their art work in very cramped accommodation. Note was made of several instances where this teacher dealt with potentially disruptive incidents by asking pupils to disperse and undertake other tasks. John was unlikely to create major difficulties for this teacher, and the Priory teacher was present only because of John's needs of personal support.

When support teachers were observed in classes, their role was largely determined by the teaching style of the class teacher and the ability range and age of the pupils in the group. Teachers sometimes felt rather awkward in classes where there was very little for them to do, and they were much more relaxed in situations where they could work with the classroom teacher. Where groups of pupils were working independently on set work, there was a clear role for the support teachers. They could circulate, giving help and advice as appropriate and this team teaching was generally appreciated by the classroom teachers involved.

Passing on specialist techniques and experience

Introducing aspects of their work in the special school to colleagues was one important aim when teachers from the case study schools went out to ordinary schools. The three strands identified in this process were team teaching; providing teaching materials and seeking to encourage features of what can be described as a special school ethos.

Team teaching

The opportunities for teachers from the case study schools to work alongside colleagues in ordinary schools in this direct way were generally very well received. When the arrangement is acceptable to the staff in both schools, it can provide an opportunity for resources and experience to be transferred from the special school to ordinary school colleagues working with pupils who present difficulties.

A teacher from Freelands School team-taught a group of pupils experiencing difficulties in the adjacent comprehensive school. There was contact involving materials and expertise and both the special and ordinary school teachers were convinced that it was a valuable exercise. They taught mathematics to a group of eight pupils, including one from the special school, and were agreed that the provision made previously for these pupils had been inappropriate. The special school teacher welcomed the opportunity to bring materials with her and to apply her experience in working closely with small groups, to this class. She wanted to introduce practical mathematics into the curriculum and to build up the confidence and abilities of this group. The teacher in the ordinary school had not taught such basic mathematics before and, while she welcomed the challenge, was very glad of the support provided. In this case the teachers had a common view of the purpose of the team work, and the expertise of the special school teacher was recognized and welcomed.

When special school staff were working in ordinary schools, there were often opportunities for them to develop relationships with their colleagues where experience could be shared and support provided. In some cases, however, the possibilities offered by the link programme to develop communication between staff were not utilized. Teachers in the ordinary schools varied in their perceptions both of the value of the support on offer and of their own responsibilities in relation to the pupils in their classes. Some schools were said by special school staff to rely heavily on the support teachers to deal with pupils who presented difficulties and the sharing of responsibility and development of teachers' expertise did not always materialize. In some cases these were practical barriers, as when teachers from Powell's Orchard School ran groups for pupils in ordinary schools and the schools did not release teachers to work with them as had been anticipated when the groups had been established.

Providing materials

Resources for teaching were brought into ordinary schools in a variety of ways. Some were brought specifically for the special school teacher to use with individual pupils, some were introduced in a general way to the teachers in the schools visited and some were intended for use by the special and ordinary school teachers in collaboration. Where teaching support was provided to pupils in ordinary schools using materials brought from the special school, the need for careful record-keeping and regular contact with staff in the ordinary school was emphasized. The way in which work plans brought by the support teachers were utilized by classroom teachers was crucial and the success of the scheme depended on how well the work was coordinated and how explicit and agreed the goals were. Points arising from these arrangements are illustrated by the examples below.

A teacher from Elm Grange School saw seven children in one school on a weekly basis and she planned a programme of work for each of them. Six pupils were seen in pairs and the seventh was visited in her classroom. The aim was to identify the areas of difficulty for individual children and to work through them in the small-group sessions, using materials brought in from Elm Grange. Where classroom teachers had not followed up the set work, time had to be spent on marking and working through what was allocated the previous week, so her progress depended on the cooperation of her colleagues. While the approach could only be effective with two children at a time, she hoped that teachers in the ordinary schools would themselves use and benefit from the materials she brought.

Other teachers from Elm Grange School visited ordinary schools on a regular basis to work with both pupils and teachers. One primary school teacher had two pupils withdrawn each week for intensive number work based on packs of worksheets brought in from the special school. He was very positive about the scheme and was impressed with the progress made by the pupils concerned, but he did not see any need for his involvement in consolidating work undertaken with the link teacher and did not know how the two pupils spent their time when they were withdrawn. He made no effort to investigate the resources brought in from Elm Grange, even though there were three or four other pupils in his class that he felt could benefit from some 'additional' help.

The work of support teachers was well received when they brought out their expertise in concrete terms rather than in providing general advice or ideas. When they liaised with teachers in ordinary schools about individual children and then provided them with specific resources to assist those children's learning, it was felt that the purpose of their visit was well-defined and understood by those participating. They took resources that they had prepared in the special school and offered practical assistance to colleagues in ordinary schools. Support teachers were often able to draw from a bank of resources produced in the special schools and these were directly available to the staff they visited.

The special school ethos

Some teachers worked in ordinary schools with the aim of introducing positive features of their work in special schools. This included not only teaching materials but also the development of the less tangible supportive atmosphere said to characterize many special schools. Aspects of this special school ethos are illustrated in the following examples.

A home economics teacher from Elm Grange School attempted to introduce a new approach to the subject to emulate the caring, supportive qualities she saw in the special school. She felt, for instance, that the worksheets pupils used in the ordinary school had been too complicated and rather tedious and she had made efforts to produce more appropriate ones. This teacher also viewed home economics as a subject providing opportunities for developing social and interpersonal skills and felt that an atmosphere could be created in which pupils would raise issues of importance to them. Some of the features of the 'sanctuary' said to exist in special schools were fostered on these occasions.

There were similar elements in the support provided in external groups by teachers from Powell's Orchard School. They were aiming to provide pleasant supportive experiences for pupils, and they wanted to demonstrate a 'fresh approach' to the teachers they worked alongside in the groups. Emphasis was placed on techniques to involve all pupils in the work of the group. In a group of secondary school pupils for instance, time was spent on completing a self-rating questionnaire and there was a great deal of discussion of the task and 'drawing out' of pupils who were said to be socially inept and lacking in confidence.

Working with colleagues

The work undertaken by teachers from special schools when these arrangements are made may require them to develop quite new skills. One aspect of the team teaching described in this chapter was the ability of the special school teacher to work productively in a colleague's classroom. The importance of appearing both approachable and competent when working with colleagues was often mentioned. Special school staff laid great stress on the skills required to support their pupils in the process of transfer to ordinary classes. They felt that the support teachers had 'a very difficult boundary to negotiate'. They said that, on the whole, teachers were uneasy about having a colleague in their classroom and that support teachers should approach the class teacher with care. The former should be adaptable and sensitive so that they learn when to sit and observe and when to teach pupils or help the class teacher.

A senior member of staff in The Priory School said that teachers who were supporting their pupils in part-time placements in ordinary schools had to be very skilled in dealing with other adults. They should to be able to 'break down barriers on their pupils' behalf and have a good working knowledge of how other professionals think and work'. She felt that they needed to be aware of standards in ordinary schools, and should be able to make specific statements about the progress made by pupils and any difficulties they were experiencing.

One other aspect of staff involvement in link schemes concerns staff working in other schools to extend their own experience. The exchange of staff in this way was seen as fundamental to the development of close collaboration between schools where it occurred. Special school staff benefited from seeing how the other schools functioned, particularly if they were not going to spend all their careers in special schools. Team teaching may be mutually beneficial and staff from special schools can usefully contribute to work with less able pupils in the ordinary school. Teachers who had been involved in these 'exchanges' said that the difference in style and approach between the two institutions was often striking. Some special school staff found class teaching to be an abrupt departure from the emphasis on the individual that they were accustomed to. They had initially been surprised to see ordinary school staff stand up in front of the class to begin a lesson. Teaching in ordinary schools had been a rewarding experience for the teachers involved and many came to realize that they had to alter their style of teaching dramatically.

Working with colleagues in other schools was not always straightforward, of course. Some of the difficulties arising are illustrated in the following examples.

A senior member of staff in a school that received visits from Elm Grange staff reported that teachers had felt uncomfortable having other teachers in their classrooms and links with some departments had ceased. What had proved productive were visits by subject specialists to the special school to examine resources and discuss the teaching of less able pupils. These had been particularly valuable for science teachers who were invited to monthly meetings at the special school.

Support teachers from Powell's Orchard school felt that it was important for them to have taught in ordinary schools so that they could appreciate the staff's perspective. They found that staff in the ordinary schools varied greatly in their attitude to the external groups that they ran, although most were prepared to accept help with children who were experiencing difficulties. Where there was a mis-match between the perceptions of the staff involved about exactly what a particular service would provide, ordinary school staff were sometimes uneasy about what was available.

Teachers receiving help from staff from Elm Grange School were thought to value the resource base at Elm Grange and its provision of useful, relevant materials. There was some concern, however, that support teachers were aiming to promote a structured approach to learning with an almost 'missionary zeal'. Some teachers felt that those providing the support lacked negotiating skills and were poor at consulting the schools they worked in; they had, moreover, failed to adapt their practice sufficiently to enable their methods to be transferred appropriately to other settings.

Satisfactions and frustrations for the teachers involved

A number of benefits were identified by staff in ordinary schools from their contacts with special school teachers. These benefits and those for staff from special schools are discussed below, and the conflicts and misunderstandings that arise are considered. The importance of matching the support to the existing curricular provision of the school was stressed. The practical assistance provided by teachers from special schools was appreciated, as the following example illustrates.

> Staff in one primary school who received support from Elm
> Grange staff in the form of packs brought in and worked
> through with pupils were very enthusiastic about the scheme.
> They felt that the packs were useful because they were
> compatible with the general approach of their existing
> curriculum. The pupils selected for this support were those that
> needed a 'boost' such as might be provided by individual
> attention and working through tailor-made programmes of
> work. The primary school teachers felt that these pupils really
> benefited from working in this way and that they themselves
> would be 'hard pressed' to provide the same resources. The
> support was viewed as a way of helping them to cope with
> pupils who would otherwise be considered for a special school
> placement.

Teachers providing support were also appreciated for the new insights into working with less able pupils that they brought with them. Staff in one ordinary school valued the way in which concepts such as volume and capacity had been explained in the material brought. They wanted more support from the visiting teachers and felt that it was particularly beneficial for subject teachers who had little or no expertise in working with less able pupils. By contrast, a teacher who had provided support successfully in home economics lessons in one school said that when similar arrangements had been made in two other schools they had been unsuccessful. She had not agreed with the 'regimented' approach to the subject taken in the latter schools and she felt that teachers, on the whole, resented her presence. They did not perceive her as having particular expertise for them to draw on and only viewed her support as being 'an extra pair of hands'.

Staff in ordinary schools found contact with teachers from special schools useful when they had pupils on part-time placements from the special school. They found it useful to have ready access to a colleague who was actually working on a regular basis with the pupil in question. They were able to share their experience of teaching that pupil and could draw on the knowledge of their colleague from the special school.

The special school teachers working in other schools had working arrangements that were different from their previous posts as classroom teachers. New demands were made on them and new working opportunities were available. Where teachers felt that their experience was valued, they perceived their work in other schools as satisfying and worthwhile. The teachers involved enjoyed the variety that their posts offered and the opportunity to work with other adults and a range of pupils. There was satisfaction in seeing pupils successfully transferring to an ordinary classroom and in providing guidance or materials that were of value to teacher colleagues. The autonomy that working in several schools provided and the sense of responsibility for devising new working arrangements were enjoyed by the special school teachers involved.

At times, the variety was excessive and could be frustrating. Teachers were sometimes uneasy too about how their work was organized and how it was perceived by the teachers in ordinary schools. Working on multiple sites could create difficulties: a great deal of time was sometimes spent travelling between sites and, on occasion, unannounced absentees meant that the journey was wasted anyway. The arrangements made were sometimes not effective either in terms of the teacher's time or the transfer of expertise to teachers in the ordinary schools, as the following example illustrates.

Peter Franklyn said that he had been keen to move across to his present post in Powell's Orchard School which involved running external groups for pupils attending ordinary schools. A typical day started with a visit to the special school, perhaps to liaise with his two colleagues who were also engaged in this type of work, and then a visit to one of the several comprehensive schools he worked in. Building up a supply of materials to use in this style of teaching involved a considerable amount of preparation and this had meant a very heavy work-load at some points. Travelling between schools had altered his working pattern dramatically, and the routine of taking classes and having breaks in the staffroom and canteen had been disrupted. When distance permitted, Peter returned to the special school for the lunch-time break and then travelled, perhaps for as much as forty minutes, to his next school. Finding opportunity to talk to relevant staff in the schools he visited could be difficult, given that they had a variety of other commitments, and considerable time was spent in other school staffrooms trying to contact these colleagues. The emphasis of Peter's work changed as he had more contact with staff outside his own school, and he now worked with a variety of groups of pupils on a regular basis. The external groups, which usually involved coordinating with the teacher in the receiving school, ran during school hours. After the afternoon session Peter generally returned to his school, possibly making another visit to talk about a particular pupil or arrangements for a group. On Friday afternoons Peter was based at Powell's Orchard where he met with his colleagues and the work in other schools could be discussed.

Some support teachers expressed ambivalence about the work they undertook in ordinary schools. They visited their pupils, who were on part-time placements, by appointment and also responded to requests for help or advice in relation to pupils from their schools. Occasionally, they made more routine visits of a general nature in the time allocated to them for work in ordinary schools. When the liaison work was effective, it could be extremely satisfying as when individual programmes instituted in a school resulted in pupils making satisfactory progress. One teacher commented, however, that she sometimes felt that she did not 'have that much to give' class teachers and felt herself to be in a 'difficult position', particularly when teachers were not receptive to her approach. She perceived herself as having some experience to pass on, rather than as an 'absolute expert'; at times she could do no more than talk in a supportive way with staff who were finding a child difficult.

There were occasions when the liaison work did not seem productive because the staff involved had such different approaches to the pupils they were working with. Special school teachers could help their colleagues in ordinary schools to describe the difficulties that pupils were experiencing more precisely, but some were critical of the way in which ordinary school teachers did not respond soon enough so that pupils' difficulties could escalate. When this happened it acted as a barrier to their work. It was a source of occasional frustration to them that pupils were recommended for full-time placement in special school when earlier attention to their problems might have prevented this happening. They were also concerned about giving individual programmes for pupils to some teachers because they used them inconsistently and to little effect.

Teachers involved in this support work said that there was, sometimes, resentment from teachers in ordinary schools who felt they had nothing to learn from the experience of the special school staff and who would have preferred to have pupils placed in special schools rather than have them continue in their classes. Regular visits to class teachers sometimes resulted in the latter using the opportunity to make negative comments about pupils. Some teachers were slow to praise pupils or comment on their achievements, while being 'more than prepared' to single out pupils for punishment or disapproval.

Teachers felt that the support work they were engaged in was sometimes misunderstood by both their ordinary and special school colleagues. Some of the former sought to transfer responsibility for pupils' difficulties to the visiting teacher. Concern was expressed about a mis-match in expectations between staff in ordinary and special schools in relation to this support work and about the difficulties that arose when standard working patterns were altered. Some support teachers felt that the work they were doing in other schools was not particularly valued. There was sometimes conflict, where teachers were required to work closely with colleagues in other schools, particularly if the purpose of the contact was unclear or, indeed, contested. Similarly, special school colleagues not engaged in link programmes tended to underestimate the demands of the work; some, indeed, viewed time spent in other schools as a 'soft option'.

Special school staff can make an important contribution to the work of ordinary schools, but the benefits are not gained simply by being on offer. The aims and working arrangements should be clearly stated so that all concerned know exactly what to expect. When that does not happen, the resulting differences in perceptions can mean that the available opportunities are not realized.

A primary school received support from a special school in teaching mathematics for some pupils. In this instance, few extra materials were brought in because the intention was that the pupils should be taken in more detail through work that was part of the general maths scheme in the school. There was little coordination of effort, however, and class teachers did not incorporate the support teaching into their own lesson planning. Indeed, one teacher sent pupils out for these sessions, on a rotating basis, on the grounds that 'it probably does some of them good and it can't do any harm'. No detailed records were kept of the work undertaken and communication with staff was on a very ad hoc basis.

A needlework teacher from Elm Grange School responded to a request for advice in planning programmes for slow learning pupils and provided staff with samples of her own resources. These were returned without acknowledgement or comment. Despite the teacher's expertise and willingness to help, there was no further contact.

Staff in the English department at Elm Grange had also worked with ordinary schools but there had been some confusion about the purpose of the visits. One teacher had initially been welcomed by class teachers who wanted assistance with selecting materials. He had sought to extend his role in the school by identifying and working with pupils who presented difficulties, but this had not been welcomed by colleagues in the ordinary school and nothing came of his initiative.

A change in working environment for special school teachers

Some of the links between schools had resulted in teachers continuing to work with the same pupils but in different circumstances. In four of the case study schemes, some teachers were working full-time in ordinary schools. In one school a teacher was working with his class but also taught pupils in the ordinary school. In another, teachers and pupils were moving to form a department in a comprehensive school. In the third, teachers were providing support in ordinary classes to hearing impaired pupils from the special school. In the fourth, teachers had stayed with their classes and transferred with them to ordinary schools. Operating in these circumstances had resulted in very different working days for the teachers involved, and considerable flexibility was required of them. The teachers involved were enthusiastic about these developments because they were still working with pupils with special needs but were now part of a larger organization. Some concern about the long-term dilution of experience and expertise was expressed.

In the first example of a changed environment, one teacher had transferred full-time to an ordinary school with his class from Larkshill but he was spending much of his time teaching pupils from the ordinary school. This represented a very different working situation for him. For the teachers moving from Ashdown School to the comprehensive school with which it was merging, new working arrangements would likewise be called for: they would be expected to teach in ordinary classes and provide support for pupils from their department who attended classes in the main school. The head of department was, in fact, appointed before the rest of the department had been established and she was able to spend time liaising with staff and building up resources before the main transfer took place. When support teachers from Fyfield House joined ordinary school classes in the third example, they worked with hearing pupils, when appropriate, but their main concern was helping the pupils with hearing impairments to participate fully in lessons. They explained work when necessary and provided extra help in areas of particular difficulty. The fourth example is described below.

In the Oakdale scheme teachers were working as before, except that they were based in ordinary schools and liaised with staff there. They still attended the special school for staff meetings. One newly appointed teacher was delighted with the opportunity to teach her class in an ordinary school setting. She enjoyed the contact with staff and the 'hurly-burly' of the ordinary school. She felt that if she did come to change her job she would be leaving a perfect situation and would regard moving to teach in a special school as a 'step backwards'. She had, in fact, never taught on the main site of the special school that employed her. Attending staff meetings there did make her aware of her unusual position.

This teacher and the welfare assistant working in her classroom alternated taking their morning breaks in the staff room and sometimes went there during the lunch break as well. She considered herself to be a member of the ordinary school staff to a large degree and said that contact with other teachers had always been very pleasant and positive. Other Oakdale staff working at the school were equally pleased with their working environment. One said that the only drawback she could see was that they were bound by the lesson times of the main school, and this seemed somewhat 'rigid' after the flexible situation in the special school. The teacher in the nursery said that she had always regarded the unit as rather isolated for much of the day and so she was not aware of missing any contact with the rest of the school. Her contact with colleagues had tended to be at staff meetings anyway.

Oakdale staff who worked in the linking comprehensive school were also positive about their new surroundings. One newly appointed teacher who had never worked in the special school described it as a 'very favourable' environment for himself, as well as the pupils. Another, more senior teacher liked working in a larger institution and enjoyed her contact with other staff. She did stress that she was adaptable and said that other teachers from the special school might find the change of setting rather difficult. She was used to working closely with her immediate colleagues and this had continued since the move to the ordinary school. The teachers that she had dealt with were all very helpful and positive.

Ordinary school teachers and the special school pupils who attend their classes

Some link schemes were established to facilitate the transfer of pupils to ordinary schools for full-time placements. Pupils were initially accepted individually on a part-time basis by staff in ordinary schools and the issue of prime concern was whether they would be able to integrate successfully on a full-time basis or not. Having agreed to accept a pupil, the classroom teacher's task was to monitor progress and liaise, as appropriate, with staff from the special school.

The pupils selected for this transfer were deemed to be ready for and able to benefit from the education provided in the chosen ordinary schools. Where long-term links of a different kind had been established between schools, classroom teachers could expect to receive one or more special school pupils regularly in their classes. This raised other issues relating to how this commitment to 'extra' pupils was perceived. In the case study schools there were instances of class teachers having to modify their presentation to cater for some of these pupils. One theme that emerged when teachers in ordinary schools had special school pupils attending their classes was that teachers were often aware of a need to learn strategies for dealing with pupils coming in from another setting. This point is discussed in the next section concerned with teaching. This is followed by a consideration of the effort expended by teachers in the receiving schools.

The implications for teaching

Some teachers experienced difficulties when pupils from special schools first joined their classes. These were generally resolved as the scheme developed but, on occasion, they reflected deeper concerns about differences in approach between special and ordinary school staff, as the following examples illustrate.

> The deputy headteacher at Freelands School was committed to dispelling any misconceptions that ordinary school staff might have had about physically handicapped pupils and recognized that Freelands teachers also needed to consider potential problems carefully. She said that being used to working with such pupils could result in a blinkered view. Nobody in the

comprehensive school had refused to have a physically handicapped pupil in their class, but some teachers had been apprehensive and careful preparatory work had been necessary in some cases.

Staff in Standlake School said that teachers in ordinary schools were used to teaching in situations where all pupils were set the same tasks in lessons. They may be unfamiliar with the teaching techniques used in small groups and not used to 'breaking down work rigorously into aims and objectives'. The headteacher of Standlake was concerned about their professional expertise because he felt that the 'depth of understanding' was missing and that teachers assumed too readily that they could teach the special school pupils. They had been 'trained to do something else and their work was at the "class level" and "subject bound"'. Some were unproductively 'over-caring' in their approach. The deputy headteacher said that it was extremely difficult to adapt to teaching individuals and felt that there was a need for relevant training for staff in ordinary schools. She also felt that they should be aware of the main areas of physical handicap and how children are affected by them.

In many cases pupils from special schools attended classes in ordinary schools without any particular preparation being undertaken by the class teacher. Some teachers did not modify their approach in any way. Teachers in the observed classes expressed their readiness to teach the special school pupils, several noting that they treated them exactly as the other pupils. This attitude is of concern when lessons, as presented, are not suitable for some special school pupils with the result that they simply sit through them, or when teachers are unaware of the implications for special school pupils of a topic under discussion. Teachers felt very uneasy for instance when discussing topics such as contraception and genetic abnormality with physically handicapped pupils present. They would have welcomed guidelines on this and related issues from the special school.

The term 'pupils with special educational needs' may serve to obscure the considerable differences in those needs. This is particularly pertinent in any discussion of the implications for teachers of admitting these pupils to their classes. The experiences of some pupils, from schools for those with behaviour problems, when they moved, on an individual basis, to ordinary schools are detailed in Chapter 7. For these pupils, attending an appropriate class with a teacher who was willing to accept them could lead to a successful placement without any further action by the staff involved. In other situations, the presence of pupils with physical disabilities may necessitate a change in how the work is presented, albeit a slight one in many instances. Ensuring that pupils have access to notes and diagrams if they have been unable to reproduce them at speed is one example. Teachers may need to make particular points to individual children during the course of a lesson, as when a physics teacher recommended to one boy, with physical restrictions on his ability to draw, that he should either not answer the topic they were covering in an examination or else should consider how he might relay the diagrams to a scribe. Teachers may need to direct pupils to peers who can be relied upon to have comprehensive notes to be drawn from or photocopied. A variety of responses are required given the diversity of need in the pupils under consideration. One teacher, who was taking a physically handicapped pupil for A-level sociology, said that his main concern was that the three pupils in his group had different academic backgrounds and he was more concerned by the pupil's lack of an O-level in the subject than by her physical limitations.

Teachers in ordinary schools often expressed their willingness to learn any strategies they might need to deal with the pupils coming to them. It was frequently stated, for example, that teachers were unsure of the extent to which they should treat physically handicapped pupils in the same way as the rest of the group and what allowances, if any, they should make. As a consequence, they felt the need for training or, at least, some guidance on how to deal with pupils. Some teachers were, of course, less than enthusiastic about pupils from other schools attending their classes, for a variety of reasons.

> One science teacher was particularly concerned about the spread of ability within his class and felt that this was further complicated by the presence of a hearing impaired pupil from Fyfield House. He described himself as not 'a visually orientated teacher' but as someone who encouraged discussion. The pupil had very little contact with him during lessons and tended to rely on his peers for support. This teacher had not been willing to participate in an in-service course concerned with hearing impaired pupils. Similarly, another teacher in the school was reluctant to take pupils into her class but this was because she felt ill-equipped to deal with them, and she welcomed the support of the specialist teacher and was willing to participate in the training available. She was embarrassed by her inability to communicate with hearing impaired pupils on occasion and was keen to develop her skills.

Acknowledging commitment

Teaching special school pupils represents an 'extra' commitment for ordinary schools, and it is important that this be acknowledged. When the impact on the ordinary school is minor, little more than recognition of the efforts of the relevant ordinary school teachers may be required. In the case of a substantial programme of pupil links, the recognition will need to be backed by extra staffing and other resources. This may come from the special school as part of the link package or from the local authority in some other way. Two contrasting examples are given below.

> Teachers from Freelands School were keen to stress the value and benefits of the link schemes for their pupils. At one in-service meeting held for ordinary school staff, they expressed their commitment to the liaison between the schools and their appreciation of the efforts made by their ordinary school colleagues. In addition, extra staffing had been secured at the ordinary school in recognition of the pupils they were teaching from Freelands.

> In the Standlake link scheme, this extra staffing had only recently been secured. The deputy headteacher of the comprehensive school saw her liaison work as problematic and referred to uneasiness among staff in her school about the lack of recognition they received from either parents or other staff. They were not given support and information from an in-service programme. They felt that they were going 'out of their way' to integrate these pupils and that their efforts were not valued. As a result, complaints from the Standlake parents because their children could not take a particular subject or because they needed to be provided with an electric rather than a manual typewriter had been reacted to 'very badly' by staff.

The opportunities provided by link schemes for teachers to work with pupils with particular needs were viewed positively by many of the staff involved. Teachers welcomed the opportunity for their pupils to work with peers with special needs and saw it as a way of breaking down barriers between them. For themselves, it was sometimes seen as a means of stretching their teaching skills and promoting their professional development.

Summary

Involvement in link schemes influenced the working arrangements of teachers in both special and ordinary schools to varying degrees. Some substantial schemes completely changed the work of the teachers involved, and many other teachers experienced smaller scale but important changes in their working week. Teachers from special schools worked in ordinary schools to provide both teaching and emotional support for pupils. They taught integrated and segregated groups in a range of subject areas. Their assistance was generally welcomed by the teachers in ordinary schools. Providing emotional and practical support for special school pupils who were spending time in ordinary schools was an important feature of their work and those involved were clear that such support was vital to ensure a smooth transition for pupils.

Staff in ordinary schools benefited from the experience of having special school teachers working in their classes. The latter introduced them to specialist teaching techniques, sometimes through team teaching, and imported teaching materials from the special school. Where the purpose of this contact was clearly elaborated and the participants were agreed on the forms it should take, such contact was regarded as productive. Where expectations of what was available did not match the reality, there was sometimes confusion and the arrangements were less than satisfactory.

The role of special school teachers working outside their schools in this way was generally viewed as a demanding one and there were a number of potential frustrations both for them and the staff they worked with. Clear channels of communication were essential. As against this, both groups were often very pleased with the outcome and their satisfaction was clearly expressed. The work was often rewarding for teachers from the special schools and valuable assistance was provided for those in ordinary schools. The most pronounced impact of link schemes was on those special school teachers who had experienced a change of working environment and had been moved to ordinary schools. Staff were generally very enthusiastic about these moves, although there was some concern about the need to maintain appropriate resourcing and levels of expertise.

Staff in ordinary schools generally welcomed the opportunity to work with pupils from special schools attending their classes. Some expressed uncertainty about how to deal most effectively with these newcomers and the need for guidance and support was clear. Where information and advice were available from the special school they were generally warmly received, although a few staff had not considered altering their approach to accommodate the pupils they received and a small number did not wish to do so. Proper recognition of the efforts made by ordinary school staff was important in securing commitment to the work and ensuring that it became an integral part of the school.

7 The Implications of Link Schemes for Pupils

A variety of link schemes involving the movement of staff and pupils have been studied during the course of this research. A recurring theme has been the individuality of pupils, requiring careful analysis of each one's needs and the implementation of individual programmes to match those needs. This chapter focuses on pupils and examines link schemes from their perspective. The account is supplemented with appropriate information from parent interviews.

The chapter begins by looking at the potential benefits to pupils from taking part in a link scheme. Involvement can offer access to a wider curriculum and more social contacts. The link may be part of a process that will lead to their full-time placement in an ordinary school. These benefits are not without their costs and link schemes can place considerable demands on pupils. The changes in organization, curriculum, teaching styles and social settings that can occur are discussed in this chapter. The need for preparation and support for pupils taking part in link programmes is also raised. The penultimate section considers aspects of special education provided for the pupils concerned and the chapter ends with an analysis of some of the benefits for ordinary school pupils of contact with their peers from special schools.

The benefits for special school pupils from link schemes

All the link schemes involving pupils were based on the premise that involvement in the scheme would benefit pupils. Three areas of benefit are considered here, in that links can benefit pupils from special schools by first, being a potential step to full-time education in ordinary schools; secondly, providing access to a broader curriculum and examinations and thirdly, giving opportunities for a wider range of social contacts.

Step to full-time education in ordinary schools

Some links originate specifically to facilitate the movement of pupils from special to ordinary school placements. In these situations, the pupils concerned have been assessed as 'ready' for transfer and programmes for their gradual assimilation are planned and implemented. Schools may have detailed guidelines for the process. Staff anticipation that a proportion of their pupils will be re-entering (or entering) ordinary schools is likely to confer a distinctive, outward-looking ethos on the school. The Priory School had a system whereby pupils were routinely considered for transfer as part of the review procedure. After consultation with their parents, they were gradually introduced to the chosen ordinary school, normally for one day a week. The goal was that this time should be gradually increased so that at the end of two terms or so the pupil had effectively transferred to the ordinary school.

This flexibility enables pupils who have difficulties of one sort or another in their early education to move to ordinary schools. A gradual approach to introducing pupils to their new placement was common for both individuals and groups of pupils. Looking at the experiences of individuals highlights how children's needs change as they develop and how pupils may have negative experiences in one setting and yet flourish in others.

> David was referred to The Priory School four years ago at the age of eight. He was said to have had a very restricted childhood with parents who had been unable to deal with the needs of an active young child. When he started school at five, he was already very disturbed and had achieved very few basic skills. Now at the age of 12, after considerable progress has been made, he has been integrating part-time for two terms and is expected to make a complete transfer when the new term begins. His placement has been gradually extended as he has settled into the new school routine.

Anthony was referred to the same school at the age of ten after a series of unsatisfactory placements in the private sector. His mother had been told that he was 'incurable' and that a long-term residential placement would be advisable for him. He had been extremely disruptive and manipulative in each school he had attended and had expressed himself through long bouts of screaming. According to his mother, his placement at The Priory has resulted in dramatic improvements in Anthony's behaviour which she could not have predicted. A year after entering the special school, Anthony now attends a nearby middle school for three days a week and a full-time transfer to this school is a realistic possibility. Again, this individual placement was tailored to Anthony's progress.

Link schemes may result in some pupils, who would not previously have been considered for such a placement, spending a considerable amount of time in an ordinary school. This can significantly alter expectations. When the possibility of pupils moving out to other schools is agreed and procedures for organizing it are established, links can very quickly gain momentum and have far-reaching implications. Parents of the more able pupils in special schools may change their perceptions of their children's potential as links with ordinary schools develop. Realizing that their children could flourish in special classes in ordinary schools had prompted some of the parents of Oakdale pupils to consider a placement at their local primary school. One boy transferred to his local school during the course of this research and the headteacher was keen to stress that the staff 'had every sympathy' with his parents; he had been removed 'in a spirit of good will' and he could return if his new placement was not successful.

An additional consideration arises when pupils with severe handicapping conditions are included in a link scheme. For some parents, part of the attraction of a link arrangement is that it helps to get their children away from those with very manifest difficulties. The headteacher of Oakdale School said that, while nobody had actually commented on the fact that the more handicapped pupils were part of of the scheme and were spending time in the ordinary school, he felt that this had created a conflict for some parents who felt that the normality achieved by their children was being eroded as they were joined by their less able peers.

The likelihood of an eventual return to ordinary schooling can be increased by arranging for pupils to be admitted to special school on a part-time basis, at least initially. This helps pupils to keep in touch with their own school and makes for easier communication between special school and ordinary school. For pupils in the nurture and junior age group in Powell's Orchard School, a full-time special school placement would be offered only when the child's position in the referring school was considered intolerable. Contact with the ordinary school when children had part-time placements was given priority. Powell's Orchard aimed to provide pupils with a secure, predictable environment which would enable them to develop confidence and appropriate skills that would facilitate a successful return to their own school. The emphasis changed for older pupils who would be unlikely to return to an ordinary school. Any time they spent in ordinary schools would be viewed as an end in itself rather than as part of a process of reintegration.

Access to a broader curriculum and examinations

Pupils involved in link schemes with a major goal of enabling them to participate academically in an ordinary school may spend the major proportion of their school time there. Some remain on the special school roll and continue to receive some provision and/or support from the special school. Headteachers claimed that this arrangement gave their pupils access to the best features of both schools. They benefited from the special characteristics of a small, well-staffed school and had access to a broad curriculum and subject specialist teaching at an ordinary school.

There were clear instances from this research of pupils who had benefited from a link in this way, either through their enjoyment of subjects previously not available to them or through the acquisition of O-levels or CSEs. They enjoyed spending time in another school and felt a sense of achievement at their ability to mix with their peers in other schools. Special school staff had to accept that pupils who spent time in ordinary classes were likely to come back full of enthusiasm and praise for the work covered in their new school, sometimes to the detriment of their effort and conduct at the special school. A young man in one special school said that, while special provision was right for him, he much appreciated the opportunities to attend classes for drama production and design technology. Two girls from Standlake School said that child care at the nearby comprehensive school was their favourite subject and they spoke enthusiastically about the content of the course. One of them also does art and she thoroughly enjoys the opportunity to practise a range of creative skills.

Freelands School provided some striking illustrations of how pupils, who would generally be considered for a special school placement, could benefit from contact with an ordinary school.

Michael was doing a full-time A-level course at the adjacent comprehensive school. He had cerebral palsy, was confined to a wheelchair, suffered from continual spasms and had a speech impairment. He had been integrating for five years and gained the highest marks in most subjects he took. Michael felt that the teaching he received was better than he could have expected at the special school; he was able to pursue a wider range of subjects and had acquired six O-levels. He passed through Freelands on his way to and from his school transport, returned there for lunch and some social activities and attended a course on social and personal education.

Rachel, who suffered from spina bifida, had recently moved to Freelands School from one that had offered no opportunities for participation in ordinary classes. She had gone straight on to a three-quarter integrated timetable and was said to have 'flourished'. She was coping well with the work and the deputy head of Freelands reported that the move had 'been fantastic for Rachel's morale' and that 'her parents are delighted'. Rachel was doing a range of subjects which it was unlikely that a special school could offer and would be sitting examinations in due course.

Apart from access to specific subjects and examinations, pupils benefit from the general stimulation available to them in ordinary schools. One teacher from Oakdale School who taught a class from Oakdale in a primary school said that, even in her small group, there was such a wide range of ability that she felt she was 'being pulled at both ends very hard'. She said that some of the children had to be constantly occupied and really needed a modified primary school curriculum. She cited Robert who had recently joined the school at age six and a half able to read and in need of considerable 'stretching'. She had to provide for him and the other more able pupils as well as for less able pupils, some of whom suffered from major physical limitations and needed to spend a lot of time on physical activities. In this context she felt that Robert would benefit significantly from the opportunity to participate in the mainstream curriculum.

In some cases pupils' contact was strictly limited to the academic context. They came to the ordinary school for specific lessons and gained little more than the content of the formal lessons. Some pupils were observed to enter and leave lessons with virtually no interaction with or impact on other pupils. Two girls from Standlake School illustrate this isolated integration. They travelled on their own between the two schools, with one wearing calipers pushing the other in a wheelchair. They sat together at a separate table during lessons and had minimal contact with other pupils. When classes ended they travelled back together to Standlake for lunch.

Wider range of social contacts

Pupils involved in link schemes had opportunities for a wider range of social contacts than they would have in special schools, and the normalizing effect of these contacts was frequently referred to during the course of this research. Pupils were said to have made positive gains from mixing with their peers and the significance for their self-esteem was often noted. The desirability of providing pupils with social contact with other children and with experiences beyond the special school was keenly felt by some members of staff in the case study schools. They felt that such contact was crucial to the all-round development of the pupils who had moved out to ordinary schools and both they and the pupil's parents lent support to these ideas with their detailed observations of the gains pupils had made. Special school pupils might go to weekly assemblies in the schools they attended and there was considerable mixing between the special and ordinary school pupils during break-times. Some pupils from case study schools mixed easily during lunchtime, eating and playing with other pupils in the receiving school.

Teachers and parents of the special school pupils had noted positive developments in the children they were concerned with. For some special school pupils these contacts provided a significant opportunity to mix with a wide variety of other children. For others, the experience consolidated their out-of-school social contact with a variety of people.

Katy, a girl with Down's Syndrome, was said to be a rather withdrawn child, and staff were delighted with the way she was able to play with other children. During break-times Katy ran around playing vigorously with a group of girls and was said to spend most of her time in the playground with a very large grin 'all over her face'.

Simon was described as a boy who 'couldn't believe his luck' when he had the opportunity of mixing with boys in the ordinary school. He spent most of the break-times playing football and was largely accepted by the other pupils.

Social development in ordinary schools

Teachers and parents could identify more general benefits that accrued to pupils as they mixed in the wider society of an ordinary school. They referred to the opportunities their children would have to model their behaviour on pupils from ordinary schools rather than on those displaying untoward behaviour in the special school. The headteacher of Oakdale School believed that if you grouped 70 or so handicapped children together they were bound to develop stereotyped play and behaviour. One mother was pleased about her son's transition to an ordinary school because she felt that he risked picking up bad habits from the other pupils at his special school – 'some of the antics of other pupils are really worrying because some of them have very extreme behaviour problems'.

Another, who felt that the suggestion of a special placement for her son when he was four had been 'a nasty shock', said that she valued his placement in a special class in an ordinary school. It had been 'detrimental' for him to be in a small school with so many very handicapped peers. There were 'big advantages' in the placement and for events such as carol services it was important for the special school children to have an example set for them. She said that 'they can learn that this is a time to be quiet and they can see the social niceties'. This woman's main concern for her son was that he be accepted and loved and, on that account, she was very anxious that he should behave in a sociably acceptable way. For children like him, 'social skills are more important than ABC'. She certainly felt that her son had become much more sociable since attending the ordinary school. When he started at the special school he went through a stage of 'making noises, pulling terrible faces and screaming', reflecting the behaviour of some other pupils; happily, he no longer behaved in this way.

Parents of a group of pupils with severe learning difficulties referred to moves to have such young people living in their local communities at age 19 and said that the emphasis should be on children aged four or five. Involvement in link schemes was seen as a way of facilitating this contact with the wider community. The headteacher of Freelands School said that her pupils were frequently 'over-protected by everybody including parents and schools'. She saw it as essential that they went out into a 'realistic' environment and said that 'they need to cope with rudeness, etc., and they can't do it at the special school – it has to be done out in the real world'. Children at this school had also benefited in that they were no longer shocked at hearing teachers shout at pupils, and they were used to working with male teachers. The headteacher felt that it was needlessly cruel to throw children out into society at 19 after having 'cocooned them in a special school for years'. She said that her pupils know that the special school staff are concerned about them and they know that all decisions made on their behalf are done with the very best of intentions.

Pupils' perceptions of the options may run counter to some widely held beliefs. One pupil said for example that if you just attended a special school you felt very confined. He liked being taught in a group rather than as an individual because it gave a sense of belonging and he felt like 'one of them'. One girl who had had an eye removed was considered for a school for delicate pupils but was sent to Freelands School. She participated in the secondary school link and, indeed, was virtually full-time at the secondary school. She was described by the special school staff as someone who 'really relishes the chance' to integrate and, in fact, resented the special school connection because it emphasized her handicap.

Developing self-esteem

Changes in pupils' self-esteem and social skills were often referred to when the adults involved with them were discussing their particip-ation in link schemes. The headteacher of a primary school receiving a 'satellite' class from Larkshill School said that none of the pupils attending had acute behaviour problems but they were all charac-terized by poor self-confidence, and he anticipated that attending the primary school would help to overcome this in a way that attending the 'overprotective' special school could not. He recalled that, after visiting his school initially, the pupils had reported: 'It's great. They [the ordinary school pupils] let us play with them.'

Pupils were said to enjoy the 'kudos' attached to attending ordinary schools. One boy, who was gradually moving from The Priory School, was said by his parents to be coping well with the transition. They said that 'it has shown him that he isn't just an idiot, because he can do work in an ordinary school'. The mother of a boy with severe learning difficulties reported that he had become much more confident and sociable since moving out to his special class and said that, on visiting the school playground, she had been amazed to see him playing with other children and actually taking the lead on occasions.

Michael had linked with the comprehensive school for five years. He was glad of the chance and said that it gave 'both sides' an opportunity to learn. He had made friends and felt that he had a good social life there. He enjoyed being treated as a 'normal' person and felt that mixing in an ordinary school had led to a dramatic improvement in his speech. Michael made the point that part-time placement was more difficult because 'you don't see the same people regularly enough to make friends and you end up just going over for the lessons'.

Moving to another school may affect both how pupils are seen by others and how they see themselves. Expectations were reported to be raised in a variety of settings. Teachers from Oakdale School described how people have generally been very impressed with the pupils' behaviour and they have been told that they don't behave 'like special children at all'. This was cited as a direct result of the normalizing effect of attending an ordinary school and they were pleased that they had heightened other people's expectations of their pupils. The headteacher of Freelands School said that pupils who went out to the comprehensive school saw themselves as successful and it certainly was one way for these children to 'grow' in their parents' eyes. They were less likely to be 'babied' when they were seen to cope with an ordinary school.

Several parents commented on their children's perceptions of themselves as 'more grown-up' since they had been involved in link schemes. Diana, a girl with Down's Syndrome, was said to have realized that attending an all-age special school was different from the experiences of her two older siblings and she was said to be very excited and pleased at home about the 'normal educational progression' from a primary to a comprehensive school. Another boy from Oakdale School was said to be excited about the move to an ordinary school and to be particularly pleased about the prospect of wearing a uniform. He now felt part of the 'adult, school society' and was said to have become more grown-up and responsible. He was better at looking after his clothes, his general appearance and his possessions and money.

The demands made on pupils involved in link schemes

The benefits to pupils of taking part in a link scheme are not without cost. The study showed that considerable demands could be made on pupils dividing their time between two schools. Parents, too, testified to the vulnerability of young people as they faced new situations and different expectations. The demeanour they presented to the outside world often did not reflect the stress and turmoil they were experiencing. The physically handicapped young man who reported feeling 'scared but excited' when he moved over to a comprehensive school for much of his timetable expressed a common sentiment. Pupils themselves could identify particular areas of difficulty, however positive they may have been overall about the opportunities presented by the link. There were demands arising from the organizational arrangements, from changes in the curriculum and teaching approach and from social situations. The research showed clearly how the arrangements made in schools and the expectations held by staff created very different environments for pupils.

Changes in organization

Some degree of disruption is inevitable for pupils attending two schools and they sometimes experience a lack of continuity. Spending time in a school that is radically different from the familiar special school may be an unsettling experience. During their interviews parents said how much they were impressed by their children who had successfully transferred to ordinary schools. Some had received all their education hitherto in small, well-resourced special schools which were seen as enclosed and protective. Moving around large schools, coping with unfamiliar lunchtime eating arrangements and travelling to and from school were, for them, new and potentially stressful features of the link arrangement.

Pupils from Oakdale School attended registration periods in the comprehensive school containing their special classes and moving around the school at the end of the session was observed to be a traumatic experience initially. One boy was said by his parents to have found the move from The Priory School extremely difficult because it was 'a huge school compared to what he is used to; he knew everybody at his special school and was very much at home there'. The size of the new school prompted his parents to worry that he would be ignored and that his difficulties would be overlooked. This boy also had a very long walk to school to contend with, which was an abrupt change from the door-to-door taxi service he was accustomed to.

Jonathan's experiences illustrate the potential problems of part-time placements. His parents felt that his placement in a school for pupils with behaviour problems was somehow 'avoiding the issues' and was simply removing him from situations that he could not cope with. He had to learn to mix more socially and they believed that he 'hasn't got much to cope with and gets all the attention' in a small class. They were keenly aware of situations he had found difficult in the ordinary school. Jonathan had recently wandered into the wrong class when spending a day at his new school and had sat through an entire lesson unchallenged. His mother was surprised, too, that he had not been shown around what was a considerably larger school than any he had previously attended.

Registration periods and other unstructured time such as morning breaks were reported to be dreaded by some pupils. Pupils who still felt uneasy in ordinary schools were said to prefer spending these times in their special school base. There were practical arrangements in ordinary schools that made the transfer rather more demanding as pupils had to negotiate unfamiliar routines and events.

In some schools physically handicapped pupils may be unable to reach important facilities such as the library and, although books may be borrowed on their behalf, they will be unable to develop 'library skills'. When videos are shown in particular rooms rather than in classrooms using portable equipment, access can be a problem and pupils may have to wait until it is possible for the tape to be played for them at the special school. Travel arrangements are a further complication when the special school day does not coincide with the school day in the linking school(s). For example, pupils from Larkshill School had to leave the primary school at 3 o'clock, half an hour before school finished. Some pupils from The Priory School left their ordinary school at 2.25 to catch their taxis home from the special school at 2.30. This coincided with the afternoon break at the ordinary school.

Special school staff were concerned about the problems that their pupils might encounter. One headteacher voiced common concerns when he explained: 'Special school expertise is concerned with how children integrate into groups and is about identifying children's needs and fitting things to meet them. The mainstream child has to fit into the group.' There are, undoubtedly, extra demands made on pupils who have special needs. Nigel, for example, who was partially sighted, was said to dislike segregated education and anything that might make him appear 'different'. He had a welfare assistant to support him during some classes but found it difficult to build up a relationship with her. Hearing impaired pupils who spend time in ordinary schools may be given responsibility for their equipment and resources. Pupils in Fyfield House brought radio microphones back to the resource centre at the end of the day and were responsible for ensuring that everything was checked and charged for the next day.

Changes in curriculum and teaching approach

Pupils are selected to participate in link schemes for varying amounts of time depending on an assessment of their needs. There may be difficulties arising from the work for pupils who are selected because lessons, as presented, are not accessible for one reason or another. Some pupils' limitations may be more apparent as they spend time in ordinary classes. Pupils have to adapt to very different regimes, and a part-time placement may exacerbate the difficulty of doing this, as Jonathan's experiences described below illustrate. They also have to deal with teachers who have a variety of teaching styles.

Pupils who have a physical impairment that affects their production of written work may encounter situations where their participation in classroom work is limited. Leila, for example, while enjoying her A-level course and optimistic about obtaining a university place, had a weakened arm and found note-taking extremely arduous. This was particularly the case when there were quotations and she would welcome the provision of more handouts covering course material.

> Terry used a microwriter in school and was observed in lessons to sit alone, quietly and attentively. In Accounts, while the rest of the class copied a list of transactions from the blackboard, Terry sat waiting for a pre-written list at the teacher's suggestion. During a physics lesson about lenses and refracted light, Terry was able to do very little of the class work on his microwriter and he sat through a very isolated, unproductive lesson. The teacher made a point of explaining to Terry that, in an examination, he should either not do this question or explain the diagram to his scribe. (The understanding was that Terry should be directed to another pupil whose work was consistently clear and should arrange to borrow and photocopy any relevant material.)

Attending an ordinary school may involve special school pupils in activities that initially, at least, serve to highlight their impairments. For physically handicapped pupils, there may be situations where they are observers in the ordinary school setting. Some staff said that their pupils must realize that they cannot have a perfect life but that they can get round their limitations and achieve a great deal. One physically handicapped pupil said that science subjects posed extra difficulties for him – when he was doing experiments he had to concentrate twice as hard so as to make sure that he did not fall over. He said that not being allowed to do some practical aspects of courses had made him feel inferior. The special school staff were aware of a need to communicate with their colleagues about the reasonable limits for their pupils' participation and understood that staff did sometimes 'err on the side of caution'.

Other examination-related difficulties were highlighted. Ann was said to have found writing so painful and difficult initially that she had developed a remarkably succinct style. She was an able pupil who was dealing easily with her work but who required tuition to enable her to expand her thoughts on paper. Another pupil had been criticized for not detailing his working out on answer papers in Accounts. His mother had discussed this with staff, explaining that he had developed a capacity to hold very complex computations and sets of figures in his head because transcribing was so arduous for him.

A number of these points are illustrated in the following account of one boy's morning in an ordinary school.

> Jonathan attends a middle school on Friday of each week and spends the other four days at The Priory School. When observed in a mixed ability geography class Jonathan was visibly strained and restless. He grinned nervously at the link teacher who had come from The Priory to support him and seemed rather removed from his classmates. The work covered was to be built on in the next lesson and by the time Jonathan attended on the next Friday the topic and subsequent homework would have been covered and a new topic begun.
>
> After the morning break Jonathan attended a 'remedial maths' class and the change was striking. The small group of pupils working independently in a relaxed setting with two teachers (one was his support teacher) echoed the situation at his special school, and Jonathan's demeanour and behaviour reflected this. He worked consistently on his task and appeared more like the lively, relaxed character observed at the special school. In this setting Jonathan was indistinguishable from his classmates and the support teacher moved around the whole group giving help as requested.
>
> Jonathan's lunch break was spent alone, wandering around the canteen area and outdoor space after eating his packed lunch.

He refused to claim a free lunch because that meant having to cost the meal as it was collected from the cafeteria; he had had an embarrassing experience when he overspent on the first Friday and he was loth to repeat it.

Pupils from Powell's Orchard School faced similar discontinuities as they moved between two schools. The special school aimed to provide security and consistency, with a very structured day and behavioural programmes for individuals as required. Children used to staying in a small classroom all day, having lunch brought in to them, spending playtime with only their class peers and being systematically timed for work 'on task' find attending a primary school a strikingly different experience. Pupils involved in link schemes experience changes in subjects taken, teaching styles and class size. The work may be unfamiliar and being in a large mixed ability group may seem threatening. Geography, French and science lessons in particular caused problems in this respect. Jonathan, for example, was said to be having considerable difficulty with French and his link teacher had raised this at the ordinary school. One of the teachers from his special school felt that Jonathan was not really making the effort and felt that if he 'tried a bit harder' he would be able to cope, but another one described the work as unfamiliar and 'out of Jonathan's depth'. Another pupil from The Priory School had been 'very upset by not being able to keep up' because teachers dictated work rather than writing it on the blackboard. He was 'absolutely floored' by foreign languages and often 'loses' his exercise books for these classes. His parents said that he had started to make excuses so as not to go to school, which was unknown for him previously.

Changes in curriculum, methods and expectations are all potential challenges for pupils involved in link schemes. James had a part-time placement in an ordinary school near The Priory School. One of the teachers whose classes he attended exercised loose discipline and the class could, on occasion, be extremely boisterous. This proved to be unsettling for James who had had considerable problems in previous schools he attended. There may be problems for pupils who are tolerated rather than accepted although they may develop effective coping strategies. One hearing impaired boy commented: 'I don't like to bother the teacher. He doesn't like to be bothered by handicapped pupils.' The pupil had in fact developed contacts with his peers and ensured that any help or elaboration he required in the lessons was given by them.

Some staff in the case study schools had given considerable thought to the issues raised by teachers accommodating pupils from link schemes in their classes. The headteacher of Freelands School said that when any appropriate 'allowances' had been made for her pupils, it was vital that they were 'treated exactly the same as other pupils'. There was a tendency to give these pupils a 'second chance' and she was concerned that expectations in terms of work and behaviour should be the same as for other pupils. Her school was run on the principle that pupils must not be given a false impression of their achievements and they must realize where appropriate, that they need to work harder and longer to achieve the same as their able-bodied peers.

Attending two schools presents challenges for any pupil, which they will respond to in a variety of ways. There was evidence in this research of discontinuities of experience that provoked fear, embarrassment, uncertainty and distress for a number of pupils. Nevertheless, there were benefits too. One physically handicapped sixth former who had suffered a stroke at the age of 12 'simply couldn't imagine life' without her A-level course. She intended to read English at university. It was, perhaps, in the social sphere that some of the pupils' ambivalence about participating in the links was most clearly expressed.

Social demands

Links between special and ordinary schools open up social poss-ibilities for children and young people with special needs. Ideally, they provide opportunities to function as an individual in the wider society, to develop personal and social skills, and to grow in self-confidence. Individuals do, of course, vary greatly in their need and desire for wider social experiences. One physically handicapped sixth former, who only returned to the special school for lunch and residential accommodation, had a number of friends at the comprehensive school and found the social dimension of her placement enjoyable and rewarding. By contrast, another girl, who had severe learning difficulties, sometimes found the social demands of being in an ordinary school extremely stressful. Group situations where there were rigid expectations of behaviour did on occasion lead to disrup-tive outbursts. This girl could benefit from participating in social situations at the ordinary school but there was need of extremely careful monitoring, as part of the individual educational programme designed for her.

The difficulties encountered by special school pupils in socializing within an ordinary school should not be underestimated. Consider-able social skills and self-confidence are required of any pupil who has an unconventional route to starting at a school. Questioning by ordinary pupils about their situation, however innocent, can seem threatening and lead to anxieties. These difficulties are exacerbated when pupils attend the new school for only part of the time. Their contact with ordinary school peers is intermittent and they may well be unable to join established social groups and networks. Some pupils from case study schools were observed attending classes in ordinary schools either singly or in pairs and their social isolation was quite marked.

The social benefits of attending an ordinary school were, for some pupils, achieved only with difficulty and at the cost of much perseverance. Senior pupils from Freelands School spoke of their early experiences at the comprehensive school. The teasing and curiosity they had initially been subjected to had sometimes seemed intolerable. One sixth former had sustained herself through a period of unpleasantness from other pupils with the knowledge that if she did not respond the aggressors would eventually lose interest. One severely physically disabled pupil's advice to anyone about to embark on a placement in an ordinary school would be to just 'be yourself'; this was a more productive strategy in the long term than trying to win acceptance by reacting to other people's expectations.

Staff at Freelands School said that the novelty of going into an ordinary school lasted for about a month and that pupils often experienced a rather unhappy transition period after that. This was not necessarily a bad thing because it presented significant learning opportunities. Some of their pupils could, in fact, be extremely tiresome and had suffered from having had too many allowances made for them. By not making allowances for them, other pupils were doing them a good turn and were helping to prepare them for normal social intercourse. Some very direct tactics had been used: those who behaved inappropriately have had their wheelchair tyres let down and their hearing aids turned off! The staff saw this as valuable social training that would not have come about if there were only one or two physically handicapped pupils in the school.

A concern with the possibility of teasing or unpleasantness was frequently voiced during this research. Pupils themselves may fear some form of abuse and parents whose children had transferred from special schools said that they worried a great deal about their contact with other pupils. One mother said that her son had 'a real knack of aggravating others' and was worried about him retaliating if provoked. Another mother, whose son came from the same school, felt that her son would have 'cracked down the middle' if he had returned to his local school; his history of contact with that school was extremely negative and he 'would get a lot of aggro from kids who know him and he wouldn't be able to stand the teasing'. The mother of a boy with severe learning difficulties was delighted when his class moved out to an ordinary school and said her only reservation was about how much the comprehensive school pupils knew about mental handicap. She said that children can be very cruel and she felt protective about him going out into that environment. She did not think that Roger felt 'handicapped' but he was quite open about his limitations and she was worried in case peer group pressure from other children made him feel any more different.

Sometimes, when teasing was explicit, staff had made concerted efforts to deal with it, generally to their satisfaction. One boy, who had a perpetually runny nose and a very stereotyped walk, appearance and manner, was said to have taken the brunt of teasing in the primary school he attended. Teachers had explained that Darren would be hurt by unkind comments and mimicry and had taught some of the children in the ordinary school a few signs so that they could communicate with Darren who was unable to talk. Staff reported that once Darren was perceived as a feeling, communicating person his peers were much more able to relate to him. The anticipation of unpleasant experiences was reported by parents of pupils from The Priory School and they felt that staff in the ordinary schools differed in their awareness of their children's concerns. Ronald, for example, was worried that he would be asked about his attendance at the 'nutters' school and his mother had one particularly stressful day with him that was related to his fear of being mocked when he did physical education at his ordinary school the following day.

Staff varied in the extent to which they felt that children who were different in some way should be excluded. One girl, with severe learning difficulties attending a special class in an ordinary school, ate her lunch in her classroom because it was felt that going to the dining room with her large plastic bib and cumbersome cutlery would not 'do much for her image'. Some special school staff took this concept of protection further and felt that time in ordinary schools could be detrimental to some pupils. The deputy headteacher of Standlake School said that 'pupils who are grotesque must be protected'. She instanced Beatrice who wore calipers and had an ungainly walk. She blended in quite easily in the special school but looked 'really handicapped' in the ordinary school. The deputy headteacher was concerned that, although able-bodied people may become accustomed to someone in a wheelchair, they may find it difficult to come to terms with an unusual gait.

A distinction was sometimes drawn between situations where pupils were amicably accepted in ordinary schools and those where pupils had forged real friendships with their peers. Staff in special schools said that their pupils may have very isolated social lives in general and it would be unrealistic to expect pupils to develop close relationships with others simply by placing them in ordinary schools. It was anticipated that as the link schemes developed and children came into contact with each other early in their school careers, they would more readily develop sustained friendships.

Some schemes function in such a way that there are no opportunities for contacts made in class to continue easily. Routines that provide very little social integration can become established all too readily. Two physically handicapped pupils, for example, stayed in class on their own when the room emptied for a break in a double period. The teacher concerned said that he did sometimes feel guilty about this but he knew that they chatted together and carried on with their work and they were occasionally joined by some of the girls from the ordinary school. This free time outside of formal timetabled periods was potentially stressful. The less mobile children may encounter difficulties as with one boy who accompanied a group of children out during a lunch break. They converged on a large building near the school and lifted his wheelchair in. In the general flurry of activity he was forgotten on the way out and was left stranded with several flights of stairs to negotiate.

Teachers working with very handicapped pupils thought that they derived a great deal of benefit from mixing with other pupils in terms of stimulation, even though they would not actually be participating. One teacher from Oakdale School said that her pupils had had productive contacts, although there was a tendency sometimes to 'play down' to her class and imitate them, simply because pupils in the ordinary schools did not know how to respond to children who were so 'different'. She was concerned about the quality of friendship that her pupils might attain in ordinary classes and referred to two of them in particular who had a very close and loving relationship. She felt that there was a definite feeling of comradeship among her pupils and would be loth to develop situations where this was lost.

Preparation and support

The central issues relating to the selection, preparation and support of pupils involved in link schemes are discussed in Chapter 5, which is concerned with the organization and management of schemes. Attention is focused here on the direct implications for pupils, who vary greatly in their need for preparation and support. Equally, members of staff perceive their needs differently and respond to them accordingly.

Staff from Freelands School explicitly defined areas of skills and knowledge that pupils should acquire before linking with the ordinary school. The headteacher said that for many pupils the main problem about going to a high school was that they did not have the requisite learning and study skills. Staff now looked very carefully at each child and were keen to identify possible limitations, so that the child could be given appropriate advance preparation before going to the ordinary school. Another school had a less ambitious, unsystematic approach that precipitated conflicts with staff at the ordinary school who felt that pupils were ill-equipped for their work and were not ready for an ordinary school placement.

There may be quite different approaches to how much pressure pupils should be subjected to and how their motivation should be encouraged. The extent to which pupils should be encouraged to attempt public examinations was sometimes disputed. Staff at one comprehensive school felt that integration should be about 'supporting children over these hurdles, rather than taking them back to the fold'. Staff in special schools whose pupils are involved in links will have different perceptions of the changes needed on behalf of their school. One deputy headteacher, for example, expected pupils to go over as they were to the appropriate lessons and to cope with them. She did not refer to any need to prepare pupils for the very different environment they would meet. Conversely, many staff in special schools were aware of the need to lend their enthusiastic support to the process of linking with ordinary schools so that the move received 'kudos'. This could raise the expectations of pupils involved in links but it could have negative consequences for special school pupils who were not selected in serving to consolidate their 'failure'.

Freelands School had a very clear policy on links, placing great emphasis on consultation with parents and pupils. No parents had ever refused to allow their child to participate in the scheme and they were encouraged to contact the school at the first sign of stress or difficulty from their child. The scheme was well developed and was seen by parents as the norm. The headteacher said that staff tried to point out to pupils which subjects might be more difficult for someone with a physical disability but that ultimately the pupils themselves decided. Similarly, pupils were asked for their views when there was any question of increasing or decreasing the amount of time spent in other schools. Freelands staff aimed to predict areas of potential difficulty for their pupils when they attended mainstream classes and made considerable efforts to overcome them.

It was clear from interviews with the parents of some pupils with behaviour problems that involvement in the link scheme had created difficulties and involved pupils in a fairly long-term process of adjustment and change. The role of the support teachers from the special school is crucial here, though pupils had widely differing attitudes to them. Support teachers in the case study schools were primarily concerned with providing emotional and practical support to pupils moving out to mainstream classes. Some pupils actively sought the reassurance that the support teacher would be visiting them in their school, some seemed to accept whatever visits were made without comment and some positively disliked being so publicly visited in their schools because it prompted queries from other pupils.

Staff at The Priory School said they engaged in constant, informal discussion with pupils about various aspects of life in other schools when they were taking part in a link programme. They felt that this form of support and training in social and personal skills could usefully be included in the timetable if time was available. Most of the pupils were described by their parents as having great difficulty in relating to their peers and they found the formation of friendship problematic, either in or out of school. While pupils from this school explicitly expressed a desire for psychological support, more practical issues dominated some pupils' contacts with other schools. The deputy headteacher of a comprehensive school was concerned that pupils had experienced set-backs when they had arrived from their special school ill-prepared for lessons. She said that one boy had come to class with a plug on his typewriter that needed a new fuse and she had seen pupils in tears because they had not brought the appropriate paper or equipment with them. A broader, practical issue was raised by the headteacher of Oakdale School who felt that it was essential to have a separate room to which pupils who found being taught in the main school building too demanding could be withdrawn as required.

The provision of a classroom assistant to give practical help where appropriate to pupils with special needs was a feature of some link schemes and the need for this support to be unobtrusively given was a recurring theme. The headteacher of Freelands School stressed that careful preparation and matching of each pupil to the appropriate class minimized the need to have 'welfare assistants trailing around with them'. Clearly, the support of a welfare assistant is valuable when pupils with physical handicaps are moving around and between schools with heavy and expensive equipment. Teachers who had welfare support in lessons requiring practical work, notably science, found it of benefit and again the need for unobtrusiveness was emphasized.

The benefits for pupils in ordinary schools

Links between special and ordinary schools may be beneficial for pupils in ordinary schools on two scores; raising awareness and understanding of peers with special needs and providing some pupils with access to special education while they remain in ordinary schools. On the first point, Hegarty et al. (1981) suggested that integration was often perceived narrowly from the minority's perspective rather than as a process concerned with bringing together different elements for their mutual benefit. The headteacher of one primary school said that his own teenage daughter was very uneasy in the presence of mentally handicapped people and he hoped that, by having the classes for children with severe learning difficulties in the school, his pupils would have a more relaxed and informed attitude. Teachers from Freelands School referred to a pupil with severely impaired speech; he had benefited greatly from spending time in a comprehensive school but, equally, staff there felt that learning to communicate with him and seeing his efforts and success had been a valuable experience for some of the other pupils. The fact that the pupil in question was academically able was said to have been a salutary experience for a number of pupils who had had very limited experience and expectations of their peers with physical handicaps. This school's policies on multicultural education provided a framework for its acceptance of pupils with special needs. The school had an ethnically mixed population and explicitly sought to promote racial integration. The opportunity to involve pupils with physical handicaps in the school was seen as an extension of this ethos.

The benefits for pupils of having contact with their peers with special needs were expressed in two ways. One related to a general raising of their awareness and the other to more practical concerns. The headteacher of Oakdale School said that, when his school had been built seven years ago, local residents had raised concern about the presence of mentally handicapped children in the neighbourhood. Many of his pupils were now attending ordinary schools without any opposition and he felt sure that people in the locality had become informed about mental handicap and were now able to see such children as 'human beings'. One ordinary school teacher whose pupils spent time in integrated sessions with physically handicapped children reported that initially some children had cried because 'they were scared of the special school children'. Regular contact with children in special schools can help to modify stereotyped views of those who are different and can serve an important educative function. Where physically handicapped and able-bodied children come together through a link scheme, it may be productive for the latter to see that the former are a heterogeneous group with different personalities and views. The headteacher of Freelands School felt that physically handicapped pupils were often self-effacing and presented themselves in a 'low key' way, so that it was good for other children to see that they had positive abilities. The deputy headteacher of a comprehensive school felt that very positive relationships had been formed between pupils at the schools involved in the links. She said that 'integration is so good that in fact special school pupils are occasionally naughty and there have been wheelchair races around the school'.

Staff involved in link schemes reported that pupils in ordinary schools were quite willing to help children who needed to move cumbersome equipment between lessons. Several such instances were in fact observed during the research. Pupils were seen to hold open doors for pupils with limited mobility and to help to set up equipment. One teacher in a comprehensive said that initially some of her pupils had 'fussed around' the special school children and had been rather too attentive. She had intervened and felt that pupils had much more equal dealings with each other now. In the school receiving hearing impaired pupils, the teachers wore radio microphones; during discussions, or when pupils were reading aloud, the microphone was passed around from speaker to speaker in a natural way. The hearing pupils also ensured that hearing impaired pupils were able to see clearly whoever was speaking.

Pupils in ordinary schools may have access to some aspects of special education through their school's involvement in a link scheme. Some pupils may 'link' with a special school for particular courses or lessons. Several schools for pupils with moderate learning difficulties ran short courses for pupils from ordinary schools designed to develop their basic skills. Freelands School had three children with learning difficulties from the adjacent primary school attending for work sessions because the special school was able to offer work in a small group; and another primary school pupil, who had a physical handicap, attended for several sessions a week. Team teaching between this special school and the comprehensive meant that less able pupils in the latter school were taught maths using staff and equipment from the special school.

One other positive gain for pupils from ordinary schools was seen during lessons in that, where teachers modified their teaching approach to accommodate pupils with special needs, the whole class benefited. Teachers reiterated the main points of the lesson and used rather more visual aids; this helped to clarify the content, particularly for less able pupils. This was observed, for example, in a school attended by hearing impaired pupils where lesson discussions were said to have been more focused as a result of their presence.

Summary

What do pupils gain from taking part in a link programme? This chapter has identified three areas of potential benefit. First, the link can be a step to full-time placement in an ordinary school. In many cases, the prospect of such placements provided the motivation and the rationale for the link scheme: when pupils were assessed as ready to leave the special school, a programme for their gradual transfer to an ordinary school was planned and implemented with any necessary support being given. The gradual, supportive nature of this process was seen to maximize the chances of pupils being educated satisfactorily in ordinary schools, without exposing them to undue risk.

Secondly, link programmes gave pupils access to a broader curriculum and to public examinations. This was particularly the case for able pupils, often physically handicapped, who were neither stretched academically nor exposed to an adequate range of subjects in a special school. Even where examinations were not at issue, there were many instances of pupils being stimulated by the opportunity to join lessons in an ordinary school. Thirdly, pupils taking part in a link scheme had a wider range of social contacts than they would otherwise have. This was seen to further their social and emotional development and enhance their self-esteem.

The benefits were not achieved without cost and it was evident that link programmes placed considerable demands on pupils. Three areas of potential difficulty emerged. First, there were the organizational difficulties associated with attending two schools that were, moreover, very different in size and type. Not surprisingly, some pupils experienced a lack of continuity. Secondly, pupils have to adapt to a different curriculum and a teaching regime that may, simultaneously, place more pressure on them and pay less attention to their individual situations.

Thirdly, there were social demands that went along with the social opportunities. Many pupils, especially those on part-time placements, found the necessary adjustment extremely difficult to make. By and large, pupils from special schools were accepted in ordinary schools but friendship and the sense of belonging were slow to develop. Many pupils felt isolated in the ordinary school and continued to use the special school as their reference peer group.

Many of the difficulties can be eased if pupils are given adequate preparation beforehand and supported appropriately during the early stages of their ordinary school placement. Some schools engaged in extensive preparation and required pupils to have certain skills and knowledge before embarking on a link programme. Most special schools provided some support, either through teachers or through ancillary staff, at least at the beginning of a link programme, though several staff drew attention to the dangers of isolating pupils or prolonging their dependence if the support was not phased out.

Finally, attention has been drawn to the benefits for the existing pupils in ordinary schools. These were of two kinds. First, they benefited from contact with pupils having special needs; this helped to rid them of misperceptions and inhibitions and to build up an understanding of how little different these pupils often were from themselves. Secondly, some pupils from ordinary schools were able to receive specialist attention that they needed from special school staff.

8   Aspects of Special Education Raised by Link Schemes

A great deal of information is presented in this report about situations where staff in special and ordinary schools cross each others' traditional boundaries and work alongside one another. Reference was made throughout the research to exactly what was provided in special schools and many of those providing information about link schemes themselves had clear ideas about these issues and their implications for the development of links. One major effect of contact between schools, in some instances, was that it focused attention on what exactly special schools were providing. Sometimes this was considered in terms of what they might 'export' and sometimes it was in relation to providing for those pupils who were 'left behind'. Special schools may be characterized by a particularly conducive 'atmosphere', by extra resources allocated to them or by the specialist knowledge and teaching strategies of their staff. These elements are discussed separately below. Each element needs to be considered in relation to whether or not it is solely a feature of special schools, whether it would be desirable and, indeed, possible to 'export' it to other settings and whether links between schools can, and should, serve to facilitate this process.

Atmosphere and ethos

When staff and parents commented on the central features of special schools, the benefits for pupils of a supportive, caring environment were frequently referred to. This may have been presented in terms of particular qualities possessed or attitudes held by members of staff or it may have related to the notion of special schools as sanctuaries where pupils can be protected from negative aspects of ordinary schools and taught more effectively and appropriately.

Staff attributes

There was frequent reference made during the course of this research to the particular attributes thought to be characteristic of staff working in special schools. These comments were made by staff in both special and ordinary schools and by the parents who were interviewed about their child's placement. Positive attributes included showing genuine concern for the pupils and being sensitive and caring. These personal qualities were said to be accompanied by particular approaches to children who were experiencing difficulties of some kind. Clearly, some staff in ordinary schools possess these characteristics as well. The latter were often very willing to work with pupils from special schools and to provide effectively for them. Link schemes have a role to play in that they can result in personal support being available to special school pupils who are spending time in an ordinary school since they are visited by special school staff. Opportunities for team teaching can enable teachers in ordinary schools to draw on the experience of colleagues in special schools and can mean that some pupils in ordinary schools will benefit also.

When staff in special schools were asked to elaborate on what they felt their school was providing, there were frequent references to their caring and supportive roles. Staff in a school for pupils with moderate learning difficulties were said by the deputy headteacher to have 'a very strong pastoral commitment' where 'caring for the child is paramount' and children learn a 'sense of achievement not failure'. Similarly, The Priory School sought to ensure a 'secure, caring environment, firm and consistent handling in matters of discipline, a work ethic, increasing self-esteem by providing access through the curriculum to successful experiences' and 'caring adults in whom they can place their trust'. One set of parents, whose son attended this school, confirmed this approach. They felt that the staff had 'always listened' and had been 'marvellous' and that Martin had received the individual attention he needed in a sensitive way. Martin had now transferred to an ordinary school where he no longer 'knows the teachers' and is just 'one of them' in a big class. The headteacher of Freelands School said that 'tender loving care' was the basis of their work with pupils; this phrase was used to reflect the atmosphere of supportiveness and positive care that permeated the school. Pupils were taught the appropriate skills to enable them to integrate into the ordinary school and were actively encouraged to succeed.

Comments about the positive qualities of staff were linked with statements about the particular ways in which they worked with pupils. One boy attending The Priory School was said to see his school as somewhere that 'helps people through their problems'. His mother said that there was a firmness, consistency and confidence in the staff that made their dealings with pupils so productive. She said that children with emotional difficulties could sense insecurity in adults and they might seek to abuse it. The experienced staff had set reasonable goals for her son whereas previously schools had expected either too much or too little of him. He benefited particularly from the credit system, incorporating a 'star chart' to reward achievements and behaviour, in use at the school. From a rather different perspective one mother said that she felt her son had been rather too readily 'accepted' at the special school. He might have 'been persuaded out of some of the noisy, babyish, over-excited behaviour that he indulges in if they had been a little less accepting and if he had seen more children at school behaving in an ordinary way'.

The mother of another boy at The Priory School said that the staff had simply accepted her son's outbursts and had 'understood'. She certainly felt that special school staff were more committed to their pupils and their lives outside school than their mainstream colleagues and that they had the time available to provide support. One girl's progress at the school was elaborated on by the deputy headteacher to illustrate the significance of the emotional support they were aiming to provide. She had come to the special school 'four years after it had been urged she be given specialized help'. When she was 13 she was assessed as requiring 'an extended curriculum in a secure though caring and settled environment, with adults who had the time and patience required to deal with her emotional and behavioural needs'. The school staff did not feel that she should transfer to the senior special school and she had been gradually spending more and more of her timetable in a comprehensive school. She wanted to 'make it' in the school and the link, with support, had helped her 'to find her feet, secure that she has not been rejected but is continuously encouraged and supported'.

When the qualities required by staff in special schools are listed, it is difficult to identify characteristics that would not be valued in any teaching staff, as the senior teacher from Powell's Orchard School recognized. She said that it was vital that teachers be positive to the children and feel able to touch, compliment and reward them so that positive reinforcements are 'continually on offer'. Teachers need to be able to provide an interesting and varied curriculum at appropriate levels and must be very sensitive to 'little signals that children send out'. Teachers also need to be 'strong enough to withdraw their approval' when children are not behaving appropriately.

Some teachers elaborated on the satisfactions of their particular approach and working environment. One teacher of pupils with behaviour problems said that she preferred her work in the special school to the four years she had spent in a primary school because of the different emphasis. In the ordinary class, she had felt like 'a machine' when a group of children appeared each year and she would 'process them' before getting another group the following year. In the special school she felt that she got to know the pupils very well and that her work was 'actually affecting their lives in an important way and is not just concerned with academic standards'.

Staff at The Priory School were very aware that, when their pupils went out to ordinary schools, it was an anxious time for parents and they 'always want to be on the end of the telephone' and were pleased when parents contacted them because they 'want to encourage that attitude'. They regard 'frustrating' encounters with parents as 'part of the work' and are 'used to people moaning'. It is of interest that, even in situations where a school explicitly seeks to communicate with parents and where staffing levels are such as to facilitate this, there can still be problems. One teacher involved in supporting a small number of pupils with behaviour problems in ordinary schools indicated that she was either misinformed about or ignorant of relevant background details when she spoke about the pupils' home circumstances. Information obtained from parental interviews during the course of the research was not known to her. In some cases, judgements were made on individual parents on the basis of hearsay information gleaned from other members of staff.

Special school as sanctuary

The notion of special schools providing safe, secure, consistent environments was a recurring one when these issues were discussed with staff and parents. The headteacher of a school for pupils with moderate learning difficulties, for example, felt that special schools would always be required to cater for the 'utterly miserable and forlorn' children. The deputy headteacher of another said, 'For certain children the special atmosphere of the special school is the only way they can hope to thrive. The underpinnings of self-esteem are the foundations on which we build.' These comments suggest that as educational provision is currently organized, separate provision will continue to be required for certain children.

It is crucial to any discussion of the particular attributes of special schools to consider which aspects are, at least potentially, transferable to other settings and which are features of separate provision. Completely separate provision, providing all the features of a sanctuary, was challenged by many people interviewed for this research. Link schemes can provide an opportunity for pupils to receive some support from a special school while benefiting from what an ordinary school has to offer. Pupils from Oakdale School, for example, spent time in ordinary classes as appropriate and yet were able to return to their classes in Oakdale. Their timetables were drawn up individually. Pupils from Freelands School all received some support from the special school and features of the sanctuary were available to them. There was an opportunity to withdraw them and discuss their progress and any problems they had encountered.

One benefit claimed for separate provision was that it offered pupils a positive experience of being away from other pupils. Sometimes individual children were judged to be incapable of coping with the 'stress of a big school', as with one physically handicapped girl who was consistently absent from her special school; the headteacher said she was concerned about her weight and had emotional problems that made it extremely difficult for her to attend an ordinary school. One teacher in Powell's Orchard School said that, although he would not want to defend separate provision, he did feel that one very beneficial feature of such placements was that they made it possible for pupils to be seen as 'pleasant kids in a very positive way'. He said that in ordinary schools, his class were the 'undesirables' and he felt that they flourished in an environment where they were seen – and saw themselves – as positive individuals.

This concept of special schools as sanctuaries providing a conducive environment for certain pupils is a powerful one, with its implications of definite benefits for the pupils involved. The adviser in one authority that has no separate provision for pupils under the age of ten with behaviour problems gave the example of one boy who attended an ordinary primary school with a full-time welfare assistant and who had individual support for seven hours a week. The adviser said that this was an expensive and inappropriate solution because the boy needed 'security and a very special setting'. The extent to which such special provision must be made in separate establishments is open to question, however. One young boy with Down's Syndrome was said by his mother to be flourishing in his special class in an ordinary school where he was given individual attention and had lots of fun. One feature of 'specialness' that was most appropriate for this child was that in his class 'time is not of the essence' so that he could accomplish tasks and learn skills at his own pace. This flexibility and the emphasis on social training were seen as vital to his development by his parents. He also had social contact with age peers outside the special class and spent one day a week in classes with them.

One feature of special schools is that they may be working with pupils who cannot be placed elsewhere or who have already been excluded from or have 'failed' in other schools. The nurture group in Powell's Orchard School often included children characterized by a developmental delay of some kind who needed particular help. For example, there were sometimes children who, although of the right age, would not be offered a place in an ordinary nursery class because they were not toilet-trained. Older children, at this school were described by staff as having been 'rescued' after 'blackening their names' in other schools. Many of the older pupils on part-time placements did not, in fact, attend other establishments. The headteacher of a senior school for pupils with behaviour problems commented that they provided for children that other schools 'simply cannot cope with'. For the older children, he felt that they were offering 'containment' which was 'very depressing' for teachers. Clearly, this 'last resort' aspect of special schools relates to broader issues of what ordinary school can and should provide, rather than to the point about potentially transferable skills and experience.

Practical arrangements tailored to suit pupils' requirements were said to be more easily made in separate provision. Staff in one school, for example, related their 'specialness' in comparative terms. Education in ordinary schools was problematic because sessions were 'too long' and work was 'too difficult'. In one unit, for pupils who had had difficulties in ordinary classes, there was a 'work atmosphere' but pupils were allowed to move from their seats and make coffee as they chose. One pupil described how much he appreciated this atmosphere: it was made clear to him exactly what was expected and his teachers were consistent in their dealings with him. Another school had a considerably shortened lunch break and finished at 2.30pm because pupils were said to become 'too excited' during an unstructured break time. The loss of flexibility in timetabling was regretted in relation to Ashdown School which had become absorbed into an ordinary school. Staff reported that absorption had been the obvious solution to the problems created by a large number of pupils having 'split' timetables but, once they had all moved to the ordinary school, they had then to fit in with the overall arrangements of their new school.

The appropriateness, or indeed desirability, of a 'total' environment is open to debate. Separate schooling may serve to protect children in the short term but it may leave them unprepared for life after school. One set of parents felt that their son's attendance at The Priory School had 'benefited him at a time when he could not cope with lots of children'. It was a 'nice place' that was 'cosy' and 'relaxed' but it had not served to 'prepare him for the real world'. Another mother felt that the school was 'very cosy and nice' and was providing her son with lots of attention but sometimes this involved taking him out of situations that perhaps he needed to learn to cope with.

The headteacher of Larkshill School was very enthusiastic about the link maintained with a primary school because it had seemed to 'open up contact with the rest of the world' whereas previously they had been 'very cut off'. The school is situated down a country lane and is surrounded by a high wall. The head said that if there had been 'a moat and a drawbridge, the drawbridge would have been up'. The prevailing atmosphere had been one of 'separateness' and the school was viewed as a 'special place' and 'place of sanctuary where children escaped'. Now that pupils and teachers were involved outside the school through the link, he felt that the school was 'part of the general community'. He said that because teachers had contact with other pupils 'within a more usual ability range' this affected their attitude to their teaching in general so that the 'repercussions were far-reaching'.

Resources

Resourcing often determines what special provision can – and should – offer pupils. This may relate to the desirability of concentrating specialist equipment and services in one place or to the prevailing staff–pupil ratios. The need for concentrating resources certainly forms one strand of the arguments presented in support of separate special provision. Changing current arrangements does of course have major administrative and financial repercussions. The staffing levels maintained in special schools were frequently commented on during this research, notably in relation to the form of teaching they allowed.

Link schemes can influence resource allocation in a variety of ways.

As was described in Chapter 2, resources are shared by schools making these arrangements. Pupils may attend ordinary schools but link with a special school for services such as physiotherapy. Staff in ordinary schools may have access to materials and equipment through their involvement with a special school. Links can significantly affect staff–pupil ratios when team teaching and visits by support teachers are established. The greatest impact will, of course, be made if a special school is absorbed into an ordinary school, as documented in several examples earlier.

Equipment and services

The central issue concerning specialist equipment and services in this research was the extent to which they were provided for pupils involved in links with ordinary schools. Staff at Freelands School felt that it was useful to have medical resources concentrated on one site. Such a concentration of services did not preclude the development of pupil links. As their pupils spent more time in the ordinary school they had had to make arrangements for the transfer and loan of relevant resources such as typewriters. They felt that they had useful experience in locating and developing a stock of these resources and had the knowledge to function as a centre for such equipment and materials. The two case study schools catering for physically handi-capped pupils had made flexible arrangements to enable pupils to receive physiotherapy. Sessions were fitted in around ordinary classes or were held before school started.

The headteacher of Standlake School said that schools like his had scarce medical resources and therapies 'drawn together in one place'. They could offer advice on physical handling and on appropriate equipment and had experience in assessing pupils. As well as the concentration of specialist staff, they had changing facilities, washing machines and large items of physiotherapy equipment. Clearly, these resources will only be relevant for a minority of pupils in special provision but access to them may be complicated when pupils are involved in links with ordinary schools. A possible solution is the wholesale transfer of items of specialist equipment when pupils move on a large scale – as with the proposed siting of a special care unit in a comprehensive school – but this is not always possible. If the special school continues to have pupils not engaged in link programmes, or if it has pupils going out to several different schools it will have to maintain a stock of resources at base.

Staff–pupil ratios

Staff–pupils ratios were often referred to with regard to the opportunities they provided for individual attention to be given to pupils and for the depth of work they facilitated. Ben's mother, for example, felt that he received what was 'good about special education' in his special class in an ordinary school. He was in a small group and received a lot of individual attention. He has severe learning difficulties and a very short concentration span so that he requires 'someone by him all the time'. The headteacher of Freelands School said that she did not want her school 'just to be nice'; it had to be 'good educationally' as well, and they 'have to ask themselves what they have got'. She referred to one ten-year-old boy who had come to them from an ordinary school where he was 'not coping'. She said that on arrival his morale was extremely low and he had not developed any work habits; she set this in the context of his having been in a large class where the teacher 'had clearly not had the time to give him the help he needed'. Freelands had the staffing levels and the ability to specialize so that they could work on children's particular areas of difficulty but links enabled her pupils to benefit from what the ordinary school had to offer as well.

The headteacher of The Priory School said that the right input from staff was crucial in determining whether pupils could engage satisfactorily in link programmes. Children might have been referred initially because they were 'sitting at the back doing nothing' so it was 'ridiculous to send them back to sit detached again'. He felt that 'if there wasn't the time or the resources to deal with them before', then it was 'pointless to return them' without adequate preparation. The parents of one boy said that he had flourished by being given 'more attention' at The Priory School. He had been referred to a special school largely because of the untoward tactics he had employed to gain attention at his primary school. The special school staff had had time to build up his self-confidence and ease his embarrassment about his weight as well as advance his academic work; his parents appreciated his growing maturity and felt that he would still be illiterate if he had remained in the ordinary school.

The headteacher from Freelands said that involvement in the link scheme had provoked the staff to think more clearly about what they 'could do better' than their colleagues in ordinary schools. The answer seemed to lie in their staffing levels and their experience of work with pupils having particular difficulties. The headteacher said that they were able to undertake 'concentrated work' as they had 'good ratios and experience of working individually with pupils'. They could act as a 'base with equipment and expertise' and offer 'counselling and support' for individual pupils. They were dealing with pupils who had 'low expectations of themselves' and could 'slip through the net' in ordinary schools but who could be 'pinned down' for appropriate help in a special school. Clearly, staff–pupils ratios are an administrative matter that can be transferred to a variety of settings, as was evidenced in some of the case study link schemes. The concentration on one site of several staff who have experience and, possibly, qualifications relevant to their work with particular pupils, is one feature of special schools that is voiced in their favour and it deserves serious consideration in any discussion of their future. A reduction in the number of special schools could result in an unsatisfactory dispersion of expertise and resources to the detriment of the pupils concerned unless adequate alternatives were available.

Another perspective was provided by a teacher from Powell's Orchard School one morning when only three of the class were present. He worked on a one-to-one basis with those present and said that when all eight pupils were there it was less demanding in a sense because 'the more you give them attention, the more they want'. Certainly the pupils had their hands constantly raised for attention. This teacher had very detailed discussions with pupils about their queries and provided them with a great deal of positive reinforcement. There was opportunity too for reflection and interpretation. One boy, for example, was asked why he felt he had not worked well that morning. He replied uncomfortably, 'Because I am lazy', and was told that this was not the case; rather it was because he did not pay sufficient attention to the questions being asked.

Specialist knowledge and teaching strategies

Other comments relating to what special schools had to offer referred to the specialist knowledge and teaching strategies of their staff. There were links that enabled these qualities to be transferred to staff in ordinary schools. The figures presented in Chapter 2 showed that, when teachers from special schools spent time in ordinary schools, a third of their work was directly with colleagues as they sought to influence their teaching and provide support for them. Links in the case study schools were also established to facilitate this process. Teachers from Freelands School, Powell's Orchard School and Elm Grange School addressed these issues in their work with their colleagues in ordinary schools. The teaching qualities in question can be incorporated into a variety of settings, and link schemes can have the effect of making them more widely available.

The headteacher of Freelands School described how some of the pupils they received were 'under-functioning particularly in relation to fine motor skills' and pointed out that this made extra demands on staff in developing the curriculum. She saw the inclusion of physiotherapy and training in communication skills as aspects of her staff's expertise but did not feel that having these needs met precluded pupils from having substantial involvement in an ordinary school. What it did necessitate was a change in the structure of the special school's timetable. This headteacher also referred to the benefits of having a group of staff with experience of working with children with particular needs and said that their specialist focus greatly benefited pupils.

Some special schools have features that distinguish them in relation to the way the days are organized and the particular techniques they employ in their work with pupils. The most clear example of this was in Powell's Orchard School where pupils had a very structured, clearly defined, daily routine and techniques of behaviour modification were consistently used by the staff. The days were carefully divided into work and reward sessions with pupils being able to 'win' material rewards and time on 'fun' activities through appropriate behaviour. A list of these reinforcers and the tokens required for their acquisition were displayed on each classroom wall. There were detailed work charts on the walls for each pupil so that they knew what to undertake next in a number of subject areas and could monitor their own work. Where particular techniques such as these are employed, they can be disseminated by teachers from the special school as they work with other schools. In this instance, some pupils who were spending time in both ordinary and special schools were on behaviour modification programmes geared to toileting, social skills or academic work; these programmes were continued in the ordinary school setting, where possible, and staff there were shown how to implement them.

Apart from the approach to learning taken in some of the case study schools, there were other elements of expertise that could be translated into support when there was contact with other establishments. One educational psychologist pointed out that special schools had built up 'valuable expertise'. Some of these were in 'pretty mundane things' like knowing how to lift and carry physically handicapped pupils. These practical skills assumed significance when pupils were spending time unaccompanied in classes in the ordinary school, particularly in relation to the fire regulations. Sometimes the elements of 'specialness' were difficult to pin down. One deputy headteacher described her school as providing 'an intensive burst of what is good about education' with an emphasis on meeting each child's educational, social and emotional needs.

The emphasis on individual work programmes and structured plans was the most consistent theme of comments about the particular educational qualities of special schools collected during this research. The feasibility of transferring this structured, individualized approach was central to the study of link schemes where special school teachers were working in ordinary schools in a specialist capacity. The headteacher of Larkshill School said that the school was generously staffed and all the staff were involved in producing work materials; this meant that they were able to give advice on and provide individual schemes of work for staff in ordinary schools to use. He said that a strength of their curriculum was that it was 'tailored to the individual' and that it had a highly structured, objectives-based approach for literacy, numeracy and social skills.

Where special school teachers are going out into primary schools to teach children and provide them with packs of individually pro-grammed, structured learning materials, there are implications for the curriculum being offered. The support teachers in one of the case study schemes were keen for children to do most, if not all, of the pack work. This could mean that pupils were spending a considerable proportion of their 'work' time on materials that were substantially different from those of their classmates. It could be argued that importing individual packs in this way segregates the pupils involved and limits what is available to them from the broader curriculum.

The desirability of the imposed structure may also be queried. One headteacher said that most of the reading and mathematics schemes used in his primary school were already highly structured and it did not seem appropriate to break material down any further. There was the risk, too, that staff would reject approaches perceived by them as over-programmed. One education officer expressed his concern that 'liberal schools' might be opposed to a structured, 'small steps' approach and reject it out of hand or, alternatively, that other schools might obtain the materials and use them 'uncritically' and inappro-priately.

A different perspective on the transfer of expertise was given by the headteacher of a school for pupils with moderate learning difficulties that had linked with a primary school to facilitate the movement of pupils. He said that contact with the primary school had been a 'real eye-opener' and had made him realize that his school was deficient in many respects and could learn a great deal from the primary school. He acknowledged that the greater stimulation available in this primary school was advantageous for most children and that expertise could most usefully come from the primary school to his school.

9 Links and the Future of Special Schools

The cost of segregation

Special schools are a major resource in the education of pupils with special needs. For most of their existence, their contribution has been made in relative isolation from the mainstream education sector. This has been partly for reasons of historical accident – special schooling expanded most rapidly at a time when primary and secondary schools were stretched to provide a basic education for the majority of children – and partly for ideological reasons – pupils with special educational needs, or handicapped pupils as they were then called, were deemed to require a form of education that was quite different from that required by other pupils.

This segregative milieu has cost special schools dear. While they have not withered away – the number of special schools has stayed closely in line with the total school age population since the early 1970s – their status is no longer unquestioned, as it once was. Whatever their pedagogical and curricular expertise, they are at odds with the prevailing thrust toward integration. The simplistic enthusiasm for integration which was prevalent in the 1970s may have been tempered by experience, but it is still a predominant orientation in provision for special needs, among both parents and professionals, and is, of course, enjoined by the 1981 Education Act. This means that traditional special schools face the danger of becoming irrelevant, continuing in existence only because of inertia and the difficulty of finding a better alternative. The lack of a positive and valued rationale for their work has debilitating effects on staff morale and bodes ill for the maintenance of high-quality special needs provision.

Links – response or initiative?

Where do link programmes fit in this context? Are they merely opportunistic efforts to survive, or are they the beginning of a more substantial set of changes in the nature of special schooling? It may be that special schools are jumping on to the integration bandwagon so that they can plead relevance after all and be guaranteed a continuing role. It would be naive to suppose that this never happens. The present study certainly threw up instances of link programmes which emanated from fears over school closure and were developed as part of a survival strategy. There were other reasons; however, and many link programmes grew out of specific concerns to improve the educational provision on offer to pupils. It is at least possible, therefore, that link programmes herald the emergence of a new kind of special school.

The research conducted does not permit hard-and-fast answers here. Its purpose was to document the nature and extent of existing links between special schools and ordinary schools. This it did in great detail. It spelled out the form that link programmes take and the extent to which pupils and teachers were involved, separately and together; it described the process by which pupils moved from a special school to an ordinary school; it analysed the activities carried out by special school teachers when they went into ordinary schools. It also established the scale of link programmes – more than three-quarters of special schools reported a link of some kind and sizeable numbers of teachers and pupils were involved.

The outstanding feature of the data was the enormous diversity of practice. Widely differing arrangements were being subsumed under the single designation 'link programme'. Some trends in this diversity were evident at a micro level, and these have been noted at various points in the text – pupils tended to move from part-time placements to full-time ones, contact between schools grew more natural with the passage of time and led to greater professional interaction and so on.

What the study could not do was specify the bigger changes and say where link programmes in general were going. It was not designed to analyse developments at this macro level. Any such prediction must necessarily be speculative and tentative. There were pointers to the future, however, and it may be useful to draw attention to some of the developments that seem most likely to take place.

Future of special schooling

Before doing so, it is necessary to say something about the future of special schools themselves. First of all, it is clear that special schools will be part of the map of special needs provision for some time to come. The widespread closures once feared have not materialized and will not take place in the foreseeable future. Numbers have dropped, but primarily in response to the general fall in school rolls. So there may be fewer special schools in the future but they will continue in existence and will still have a contribution to make to the education of pupils with special needs.

But what will they look like? The assumption has to be that there will be considerable changes and that special schools of the future will be quite different from those of today. Hegarty (1987) points out some of the more visible changes that can be expected – greater use of technology, especially computer-based technology; schools built and fitted out to a higher standard; possibly more residential accommodation as the number of special schools gets fewer and pupils have longer distances to travel to them. If ordinary schools cater for a greater proportion of pupils with special needs, special schools will have a different clientele: they will be left with those who have the greatest and most complex learning difficulties and will have to adapt their teaching approaches and develop their resources accordingly.

The most significant changes will be the structural ones. These will derive partly from the differences in the client group and partly from the wider range of functions that special schools will take on. If special schools are dealing primarily with pupils who have severe and complex special needs, the established school groupings in terms of the traditional categories of handicap – blindness, physical handicap, educational subnormality and so on – will have less relevance since so many pupils will exhibit difficulties that fall into several different categories. This will lead to special schools which are organized quite differently from present day special schools. Schools might operate, for instance, on an area basis, catering for all pupils in the neighbourhood with a wide range of special educational needs, or they might attempt to organise themselves in terms of a new mapping of special educational need that was geared directly to pupils' requirement of specialist teaching.

Major structural changes will be forced on special schools as a result of new functions they will take on. These will arise from both professional and service requirements as schools and local authorities seek to build up provision for pupils with special needs on the basis of developed expertise. These new functions could include: contributing to specialized assessments as part of the multi-professional assessments required by the 1981 Act; acting as an information exchange on special needs, evaluating and disseminating information on equipment, computer software and other specialist resources; organizing and contributing to local in-service training activities; providing concentrated experience of pupils with special needs for those who wish to specialize in teaching them; developing aspects of the curriculum for pupils with particular learning difficulties and field testing new developments in controlled settings; and providing advice and consultation on a wide range of matters relating to the education of pupils with special needs.

These, or similar functions, will shape the special school of the future. The list could well be modified or extended, since the future cannot be foretold with certainty. Some schools indeed might claim to be engaged in them already. However the listing is modified, the broadening of the special school that will certainly take place provides an essential context within which link programmes must be viewed.

Links as temporary

This perspective would suggest that link programmes are a temporary phenomenon only. They carry within them the seeds of their own destruction in that, if they are successful, they become superfluous. Consider pupil link programmes first, since the most prevalent form of link consists of pupils from a special school spending part of their time at an ordinary school, usually with some initial staff support from the special school. These programmes are based on feeding out to ordinary schools those pupils who can be educated satisfactorily, for at least part of the time, in an ordinary school. Placements are usually part-time to begin with. In some cases, the objective is to build up to a full-time placement and transfer to the ordinary school roll. Even where this is not the goal, substantial part-time placements may be secured and the exact role of the special school deserves scrutiny. Support may be provided by the special school at the outset but, in the long term, any necessary support must be established within the ordinary school as an integral part of it. When this is done successfully, there are two outcomes: special schools will have transferred all the pupils that can readily be transferred and will have remaining only pupils with severe and complex difficulties; and ordinary schools will have built up the requisite support structures.

There is no place for pupil link programmes in such a scenario. Ordinary schools are better placed than before to educate pupils with special needs and will not seek special school placements for so many of their pupils, so that the potential candidates for returning to an ordinary school via a link programme will not have left the ordinary school in the first place. By the same token, the pupils remaining in special schools are not ready candidates for such programmes and quite different strategies may be needed to secure their participation in an ordinary school.

Teacher links become equally redundant, for broadly similar reasons. The cumulative effect of pupil link programmes is to make the expertise of special schools less relevant to the needs of ordinary schools. If special schools are concerned exclusively with pupils having severe and complex learning difficulties, their teachers will be specialists, drawing on highly specific professional backgrounds and working in tightly structured settings. This means that they will have less to contribute to ordinary schools. Their knowledge and skills will have limited overlap with the knowledge and skills required of teachers in ordinary schools dealing with pupils who have special educational needs, and the latter in their turn will have less need of the expertise residing in special schools.

Alternative scenarios

The drawback with this scenario is that it is too cut-and-dried. It is also detached from reality. It assumes that provision develops according to a rational pattern, that initiatives will be followed through to their logical conclusion and that the pace of change will be relatively homogeneous across the education system. None of these assumptions is likely to hold in practice. The emergence of link programmes to date is as haphazard as the establishment of special schools and their deployment by local authorities have been. Despite the number of special schools engaged in link programmes, the diversity of such programmes has been much in evidence.

Two alternative scenarios can therefore be envisaged, one pessimistic and one optimistic. The pessimistic scenario follows from the observation that many link programmes are in fact very modest and impinge little on the life of the special school concerned. It is easy to imagine such links fading out and special schools reverting to their erstwhile isolation. It may be, for instance, that special school teachers deem the potential gains not be commensurate with the time and effort entailed or ordinary schools may, in an era of contractual duties, decide that servicing link programmes is not part of their work. In either case, the result will be that link programmes turn out to be no more than an interesting footnote in the history of provision for special needs.

A more optimistic scenario is where link programmes are part of the dynamic for change. Some of the new functions posited for special schools above are themselves a form of link, for example giving advice on matters relating to the education of pupils with special needs. To the extent that such links are pursued, they are changing special schools – in terms of expertise required, deployment of staff and, above all, outlook. Other new functions make most sense, and are achieved most effectively if they are carried out within a network of linking schools. These include contributing to in-service training activities and acting as an information exchange on curriculum and resources relating to special needs. If, for example, a special school provides sustained in-service training for staff in local primary and secondary schools, it will certainly change both internally and in its relationships to neighbourhood schools.

There are other functions which, at first glance, do not bear on link programmes but which do, in fact, illustrate their dynamic nature. Take assessment, for instance. Special schools can contribute to the assessments that local authorities need to carry out, particularly when children have complex learning difficulties, by supplying specific expertise in, for example, visual impairment or by providing short-term diagnostic placements. If special schools offer such a service, they are thereby forging links with agencies outside the school, though not necessarily with many ordinary schools. They are also helping to raise their profile in the local education community and establish themselves as a source of expertise in special needs. This has a cumulative effect. The more visible they are, the greater the likelihood that their expertise will be called upon. So, what starts out as a one-off response to a request for help with a placement decision can build up to a situation where the special school has to be restructured to allow for a significant role in the local authority's assessment procedures.

The full impact of link programmes on special schooling is not discerned by looking at the individual new functions that special school might take on. A broader picture comes from looking at the total pattern of change in schools. If all the potential developments come to fruition, special schools of the future will be quite different institutions. Hegarty (1987) suggests that they will need to 'comprise elements of teachers' centre, the advisory service and the pilot project', as well as other strands that do not have current institutional analogues in the world of education.

It is impossible to predict what exactly will happen or which elements will be given priority, but it is likely that link programmes will play a key part in the process. Their significance extends well beyond the particular sets of links to which they can rise. By thrusting new functions on special schools and opening up new relationships with the local education community, link programmes are an essential element of the dynamic for change and will be a major force in shaping the future of special schooling.

References

HEGARTY, S. (1987). *Meeting Special Needs in Ordinary Schools.* London: Cassell.

HEGARTY, S. and MOSES, D. (Eds) (1988). *Developing Expertise – INSET for special educational needs.* Windsor: NFER-NELSON.

HEGARTY, S. and POCKLINGTON, K. with LUCAS, D. (1981). *Educating Pupils with Special Needs in the Ordinary School.* Windsor: NFER-NELSON

MOSES, D., HEGARTY, S. and JOWETT, S. (1988). *Supporting Ordinary Schools: LEA initiatives.* Windsor: NFER-NELSON.

ROBSON, C., SEBBA, J., MITTLER, P. and DAVIES, G. (1988). *In-service Training and Special Educational Needs: Running Short School-focussed Courses.* Manchester: Manchester University Press.

SWANN, W. (1985). 'Is the integration of children with special needs happening?', *Oxford Review of Education*, 11, 1, 3–18.

WARNOCK REPORT. GREAT BRITAIN. DEPARTMENT OF EDUCATION AND SCIENCE (1978). *Special Educational Needs. Report of the Committee of Enquiry into the Education of Handicapped Children and Young People.* London: HMSO.

THE NFER RESEARCH LIBRARY

Titles available in the NFER Research Library

	HARDBACK	SOFTBACK
TITLE	*ISBN*	*ISBN*
Joining Forces: a study of links between special and ordinary schools (Jowett, Hegarty, Moses)	0 7005 1179 2	0 7005 1162 8
Supporting Ordinary Schools: LEA initiatives (Moses, Hegarty, Jowett)	0 7005 1177 6	0 7005 1163 6
Developing Expertise: INSET for special educational needs (Moses and Hegarty (Eds))	0 7005 1178 4	0 7005 1164 4

Further titles report research into *Graduated Tests in Mathematics for Lower Attaining Pupils in Secondary Schools; Course Teams in Further Education; LEA Instrumental Music Provision; LEA Advisers* and *The Role of the Mathematics Coordinator in Primary and Middle Schools.*

Other reports based on NFER research and published by NFER-NELSON

	HARDBACK	SOFTBACK
TITLE	*ISBN*	*ISBN*
Secondary Headship: The First Years (Weindling, Earley)	—	0 7005 1071 0
YTS: The Impact on FE (Stoney, Lines)	—	0 7005 1151 2
Choosing Schools: Parents, LEAs and the 1980 Education Act (Stillman, Maychell)	—	0 7005 1069 9
Aspects of Science Education in English Schools (Keys)	0 7005 1074 5	—
The Study of Written Composition in England and Wales (Gorman, Gubb, Price)	0 7005 1075 3	—
The Second International Mathematics Study in England and Wales (Cresswell, Gubb)	0 7005 1128 8	—

For further information contact the Customer Support Department, NFER-NELSON, Darville House, 2 Oxford Road East, Windsor, Berks SL4 1DF, England. Tel: (0753) 858961   Telex 937400 ONECOM G Ref. 24966001